MADE BY HAND

CONTEMPORARY MAKERS, TRADITIONAL PRACTICES

black dog
publishing

london uk

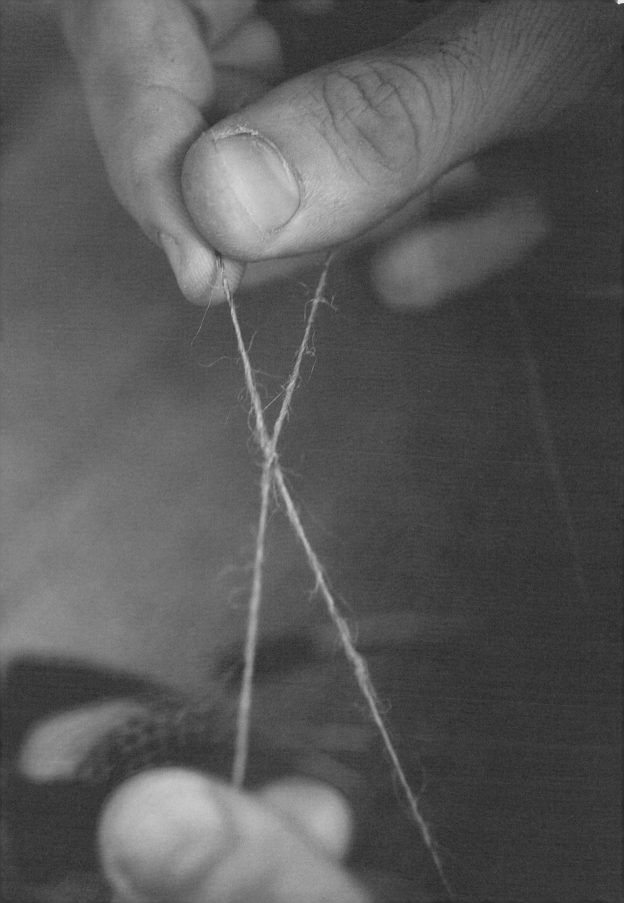

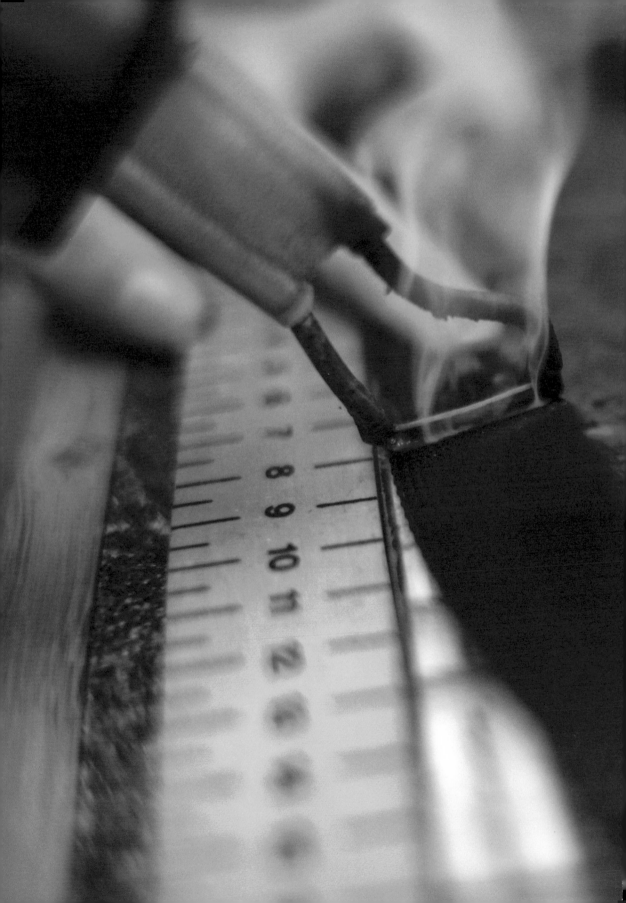

INTRODUCTION

In recent years, handmade products have enjoyed a growing popularity as the result of a changing global understanding of manufacturing and production. There are several reasons why.

The first is ecological. Manufacturing, mass-production, import and export, and a massive rise in the use of synthetic materials are all symptoms of an increasingly globalised society, one inherently dependent on those fossil fuels that are detrimental to our planet's well-being. Having more makers making products for fewer customers on a smaller scale is inevitably less impactful on the planet's ecology than big brand, industrial manufacturing. Makers that are producing products on a more intimate basis for local buyers have a much lighter carbon footprint, independent as they are of shipping their goods worldwide. Using materials purchased from local farmers and producers and selling within a community is obviously a huge boost for local economies too.

The second is financial hardship induced frugality. The greater quality and longevity of hand crafted and individually finished products are important factors in an increasingly thrifty market. Global capitalism has taught us that the economy is king, and that inexpensive, easily manufactured products are the future. Poorly made, quick to produce and ultimately disposable products are filling up our homes as we continue to buy, discard and replace them. A quality handmade product however, while costing several times more, may last a lifetime. This is a popular attribute with consumers spending their money with greater consideration since the last economic downturn.

More important than either of these factors, perhaps, is the feeling one gets from engaging with handmade products and their makers. In a society of widespread homogeneity, where you often see someone wearing an outfit identical to your own, where your most prized possessions were probably made by the underpaid and overworked several thousand miles away, it feels exciting to have something different, something unique, and something 'clean'. We are engaged and entertained by the notion that we can actually meet, face-to-face, the maker of our suit, bike or shoes; that we might discuss with them how the product will be made, and how its making will be adapted to suit our exacting requirements.

Made by Hand features some of the world's finest hand makers. Some profiles focus on a company or collective, some on a lone individual. Some featured makers have been practising their trade for many years, stoically crafting their product, indifferent or unaware of hand crafting's fluctuating popularity. Some of those detailed here are young makers, rising stars only a few years into their careers, symptomatic of the public's new penchant for all things handmade. But there are several things that unite the disparate contributors in *Made by Hand*: their exquisite craft, their undying loyalty to their discipline, and their absolute commitment to using traditional materials and traditional techniques to help push contemporary design in new directions.

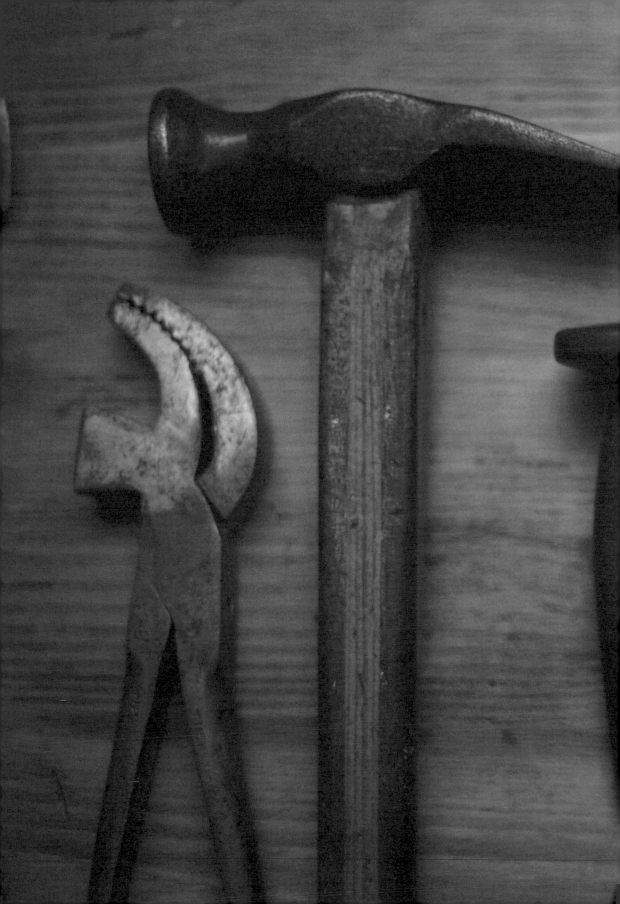

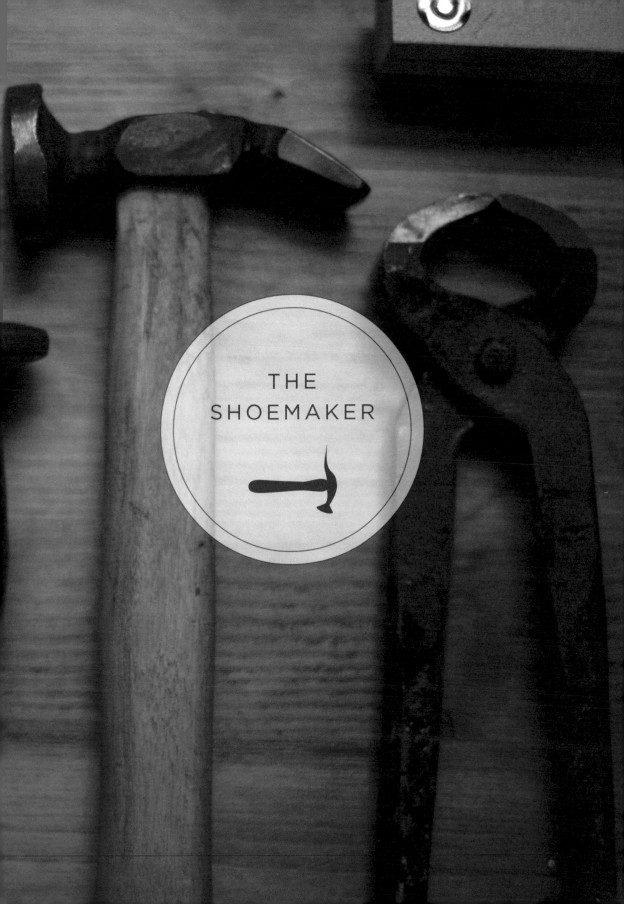

THE
SHOEMAKER

"I'm in the process of manufacturing my own leather from sheep pelts, we had some sheep on the farm that recently went to slaughter and I am going to tan the leather using oak bark from the woods and make some shoes from them."

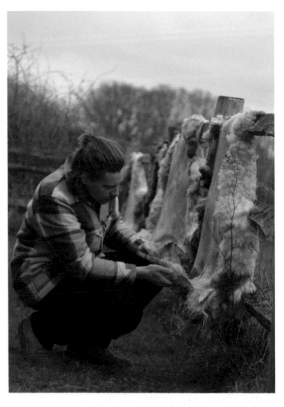

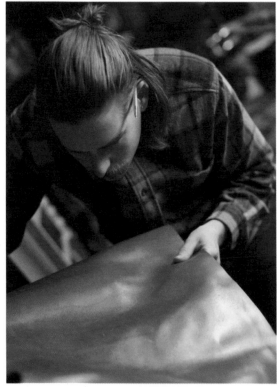

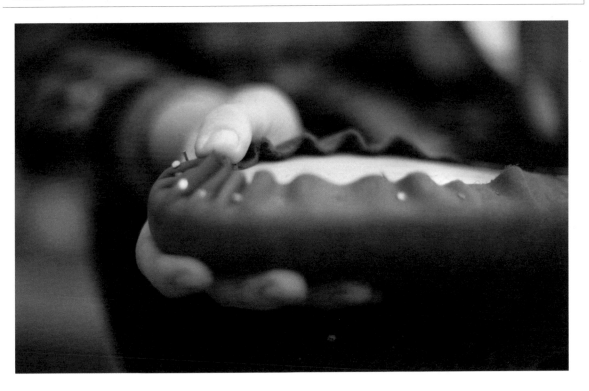

EAST SUSSEX, UNITED KINGDOM

ALEXANDER REED

Towards the end of Alexander Reed's degree in photography he started to grow weary of the 'conceptual', and felt increasingly drawn to the idea of working with his hands. A short lived but passionate affair with picture framing followed, but Alexander found that he wanted more—to work on hand crafted products for longer, to develop closer relationships with his clients, and to work with a broader variety of more malleable materials.

Working closely with clients is the primary concern of Alexander's practice. He believes completely that this is what consumers want too, to know the maker who is producing their product personally, to converse with them at length about the development of their product. "This is a far cry from decades of manufacturing being outsourced abroad to large factories, where there is no relationship between the maker and the end user."

Alexander learnt his trade, after having abandoned picture framing, at a small London shoemaker, T&F Slack. They took him on with out him having had any experience of shoe making whatsoever. He studied hard

for three years, first hand shaping each leather upper around a wooden last, and later overseeing the production of multiple pairs of shoes in a factory full of modern machinery. It was a year ago that Alexander left T&F Slack and started making his own shoes out of premises in rural Sussex.

There are three reasons Alexander has decided to invest in hand making as a culture, the first is the customers-to-maker relationship already mentioned. The second is uniqueness. With mass-manufacture and the high street being dominated by a small group of big-brand retailers, fashion is becoming increasingly homogenised—as Alexander puts it, "who wants to own a printed garment from the high street that you might see another three people wearing that same day?" The third reason is economy. With a general public feeling strapped for cash and more cautious about their purchases, there is much more room for products that, although being more expensive, will last a lifetime.

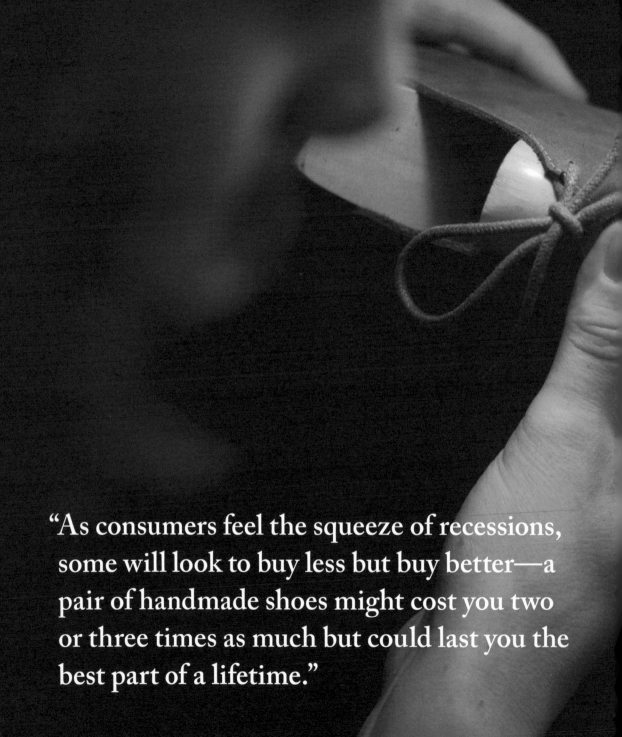

"As consumers feel the squeeze of recessions, some will look to buy less but buy better—a pair of handmade shoes might cost you two or three times as much but could last you the best part of a lifetime."

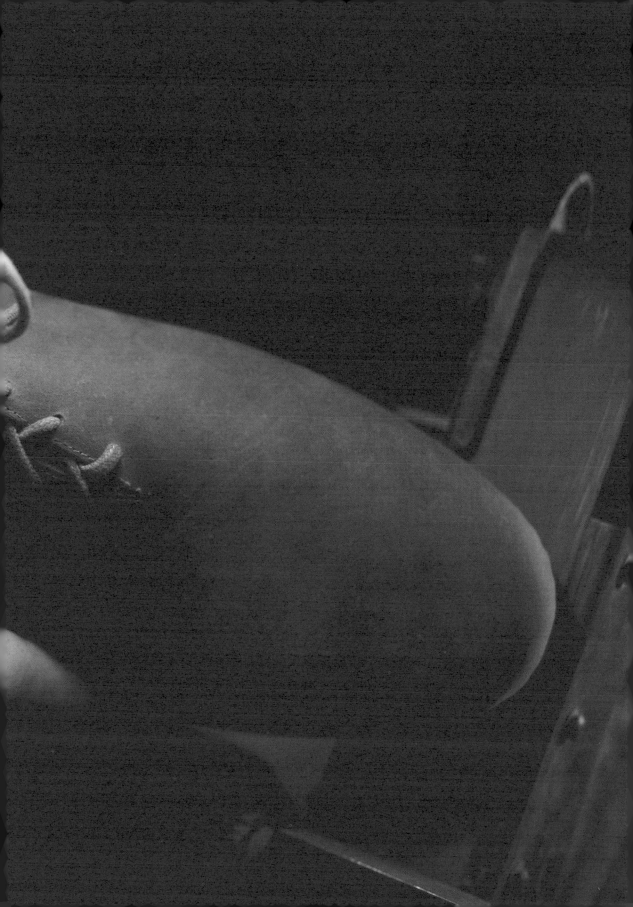

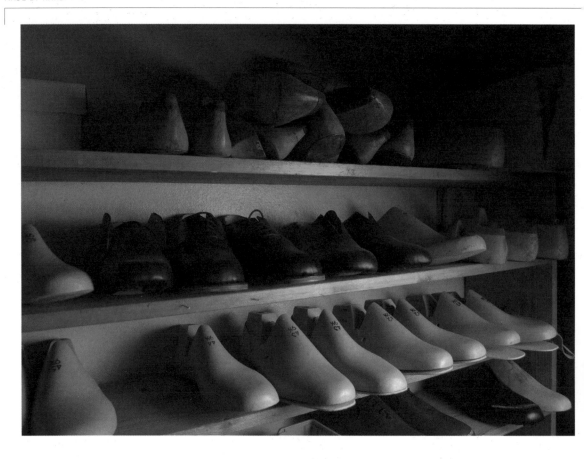

SKELLEFTEÅ, SWEDEN

VIKTORIA NILSSON

Some of Viktoria Nilsson's earliest memories are of polishing shoes in her father's cobbler's shop in Skellefteå, northern Sweden. Following his example, and her grandfather's before him, Viktoria is now the third generation of shoemaker in the family, operating from a small corner of her father's workshop.

Though she studied at contemporary schools of fashion including London College of Fashion, Viktoria handcrafts shoes using highly traditional techniques, her contribution to keeping alive an increasingly rare trade. Entirely handmade by her, from the initial design to the final product, the process includes cutting and pinning together parts, before leaving the skins to settle on lasts —a wooden foot-shaped form—for a week or so.

Viktoria's simple designs are inspired by nature and made with natural materials including salmon skin, which she tans herself using a traditional recipe of olive oil, egg yolk and soap; recycled leather products; natural vegetable-tanned leather; and reindeer skin. Using these resources makes durable, comfortable, high-quality shoes while supporting both the indigenous Scandinavian Sami people, whose main source of income is Reindeer hearding, and one of the oldest tanneries in northern Sweden—another third generation family business like her own.

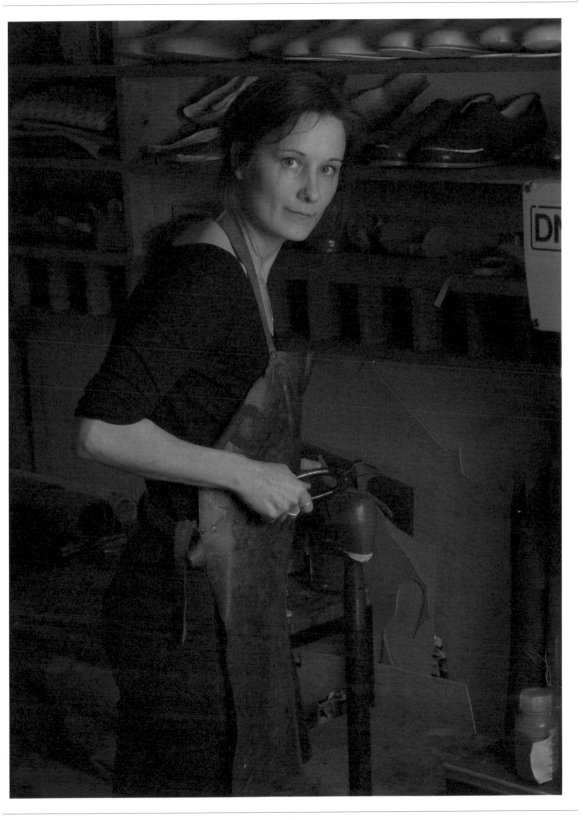

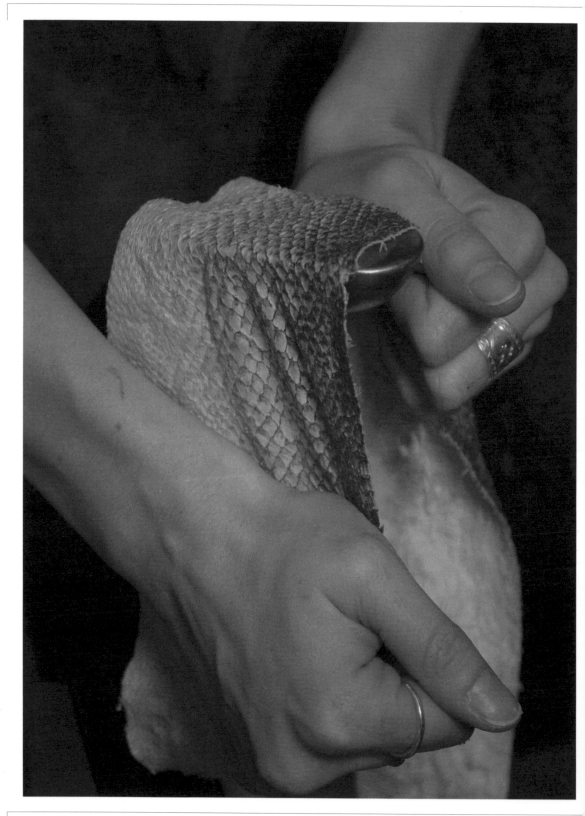

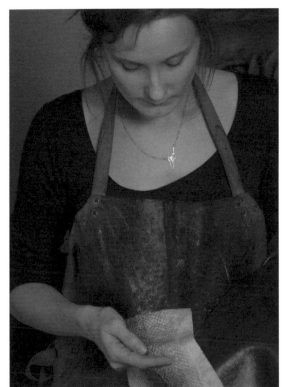

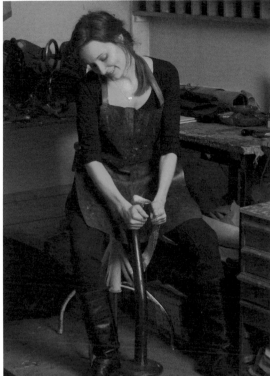

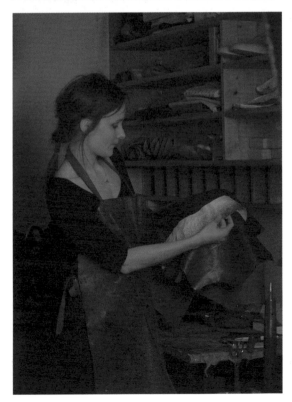

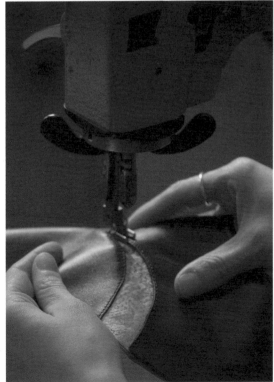

"I feel it is very important to preserve a handcraftmanship that is disappearing more and more, and that is one of the reason why I do the clicking and closing, and lasting myself."

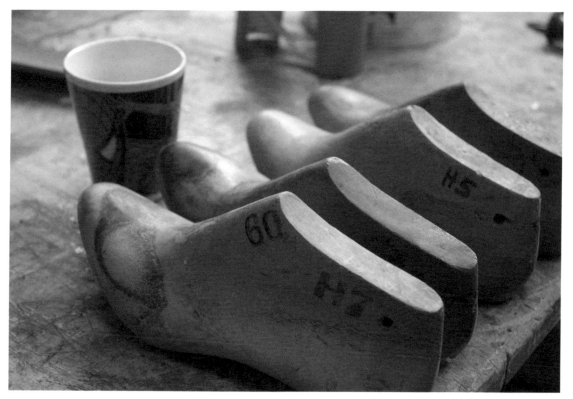

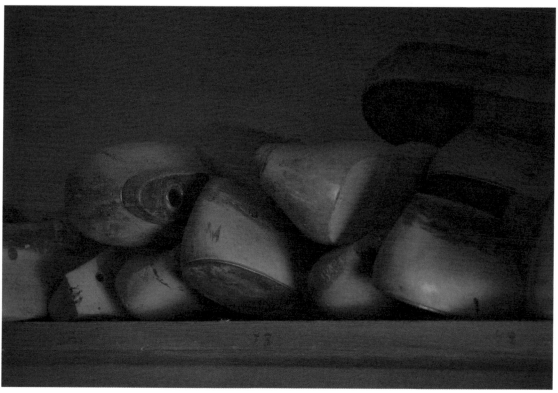

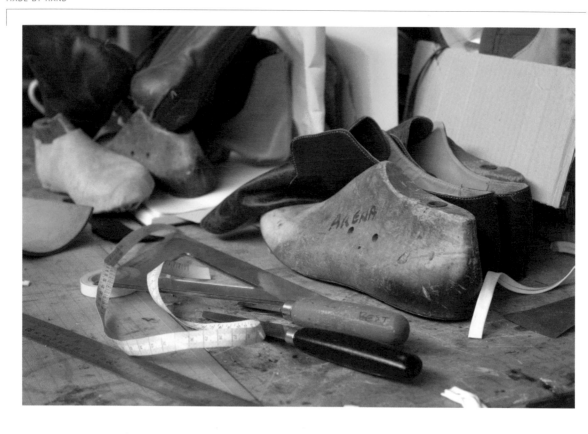

CLAIRE BEST

Claire Best designs and hand makes bespoke men's and women's footwear. Having completed several shoe design courses, Claire started her own practice and now also teaches the trade to nascent Melbourne-based shoe making novices. Claire's practice balances tradition with contemporary design, giving prominence to the quality of both the materials and the craftsmanship. Typically involving a series of consultations and fittings, each finished pair is entirely unique and customised to fit the client perfectly.

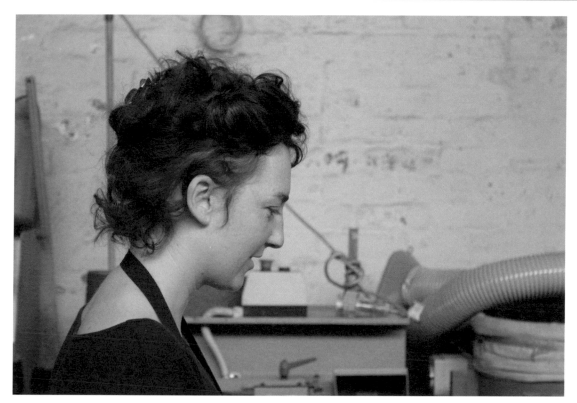

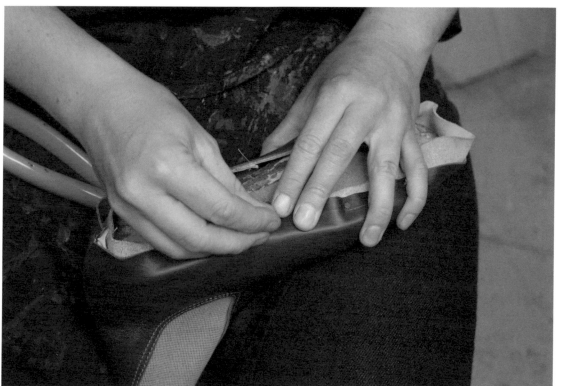

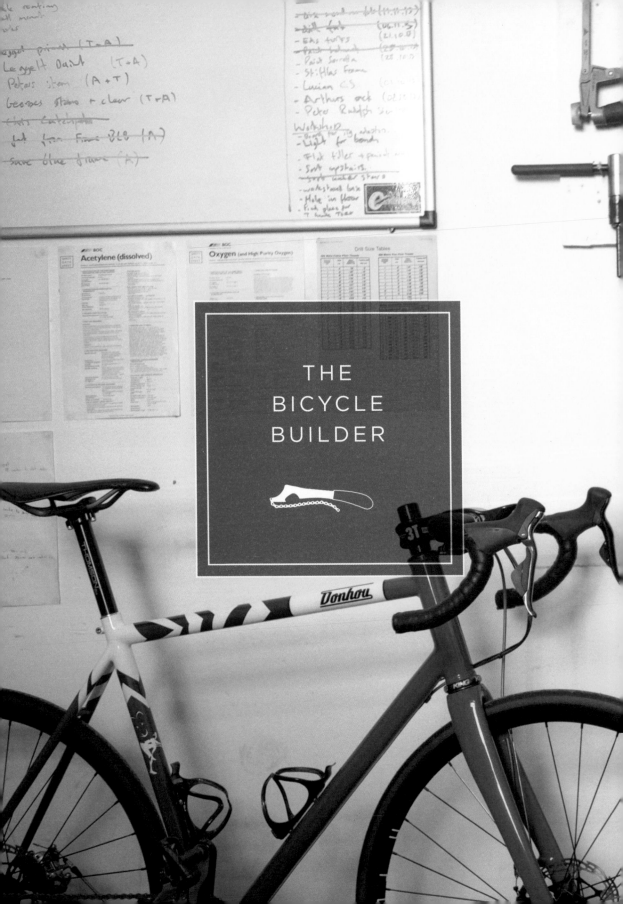

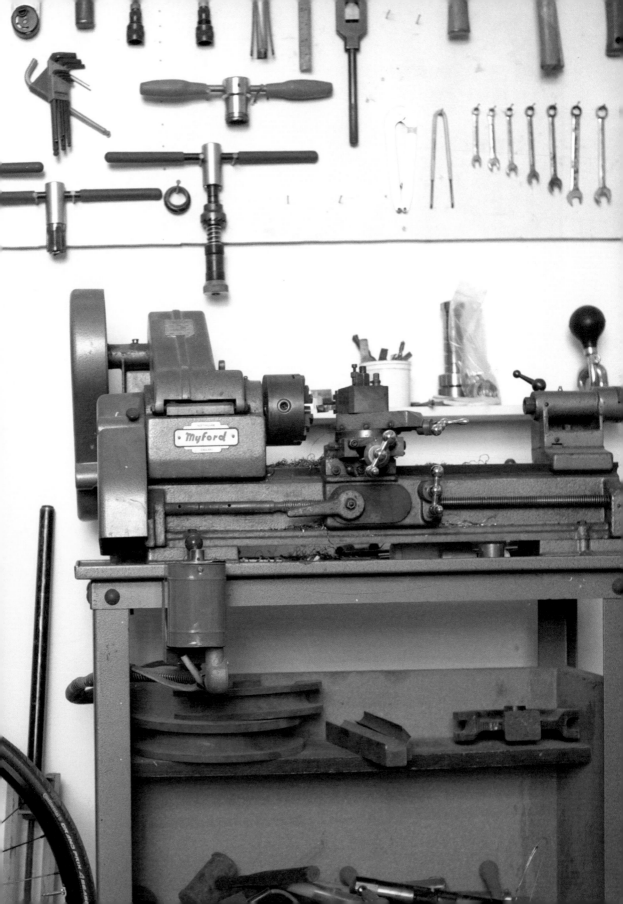

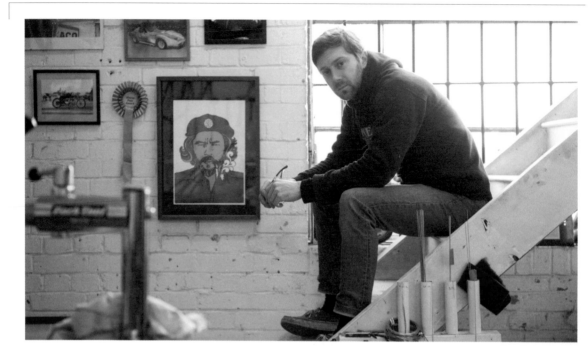

DONHOU CYCLES

Previous to Donhou Cycles, Tom Donhou was working for a product design company, designing perfume bottles and gift packaging for high street retailers. The dispensability and waste involved in this line of work made him uncomfortable however, whilst the work itself didn't challenge his design sense enough. Having quit his job, he went travelling, driving on land all the way to Mongolia, and then cycling onwards, out into the Gobi Desert, down through China, Vietnam, Laos, Thailand, Malaysia, and finally arriving in Singapore. Throughout his travels, Donhou redesigned and reworked his bike, increasing comfort and bettering its ability to deal with the different riding conditions he encountered. It soon became apparent that designing and building bikes is what he should do upon his return to the United Kingdom, which he did, launching Donhou Cycles soon after.

Donhou's lifelong affinity with cycling shows through in his work, having been a cycling enthusiast since childhood, variously interested in BMXing, mountain bike racing and road riding. Donhou's bikes are lovingly built from steel, the material that receives the most attention from the handmade bicycle community, due to its durability, workability and uncompromisingly excellent feel of the ride. His frames follow a sort of classic aesthetic, with contemporary twists throughout.

Why the sudden resurgence in handmade products? Donhou tells us it's for the same reason that cycling is enjoying a new upsurge of interest. People, globally, are becoming aware of environmental issues, healthy living, and the value of a local as opposed to a global economy. Global capitals are becoming more and more cycle friendly, taking the lead from cities like Copenhagen and Amsterdam. With one-man operations like Donhou Cycles your bike will be built by a single set of hands, not a factory full of workers, taking around two weeks from start to finish.

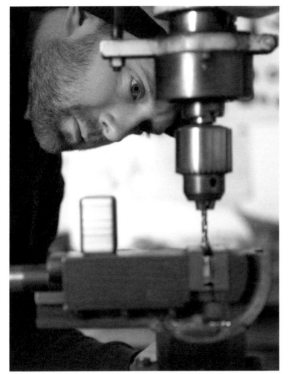

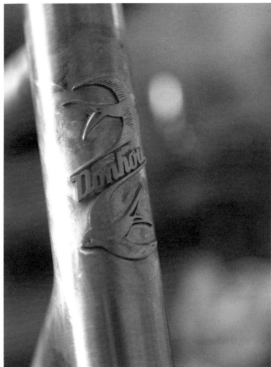

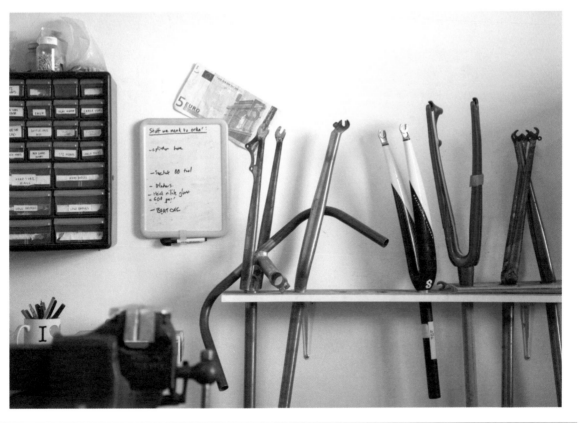

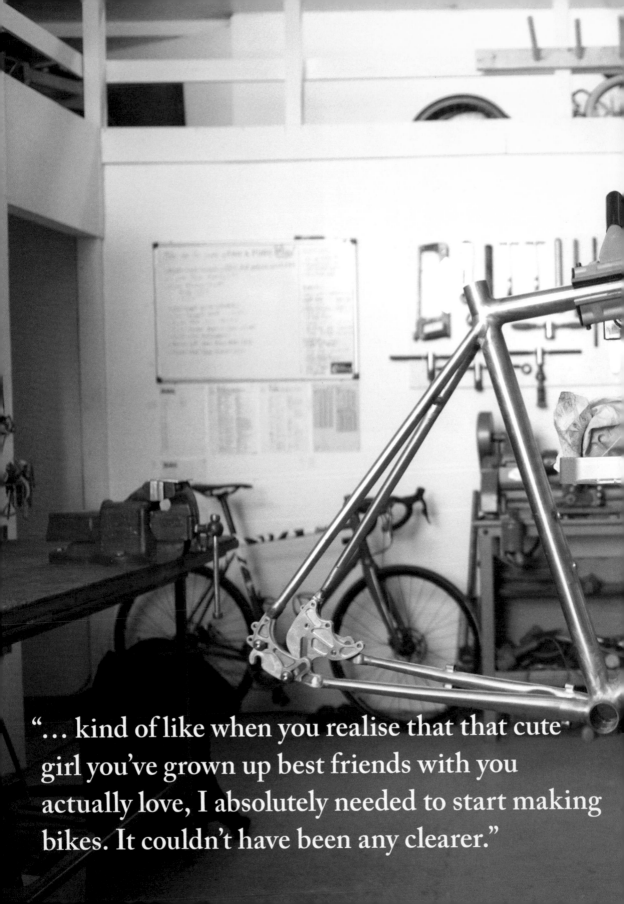

"… kind of like when you realise that that cute girl you've grown up best friends with you actually love, I absolutely needed to start making bikes. It couldn't have been any clearer."

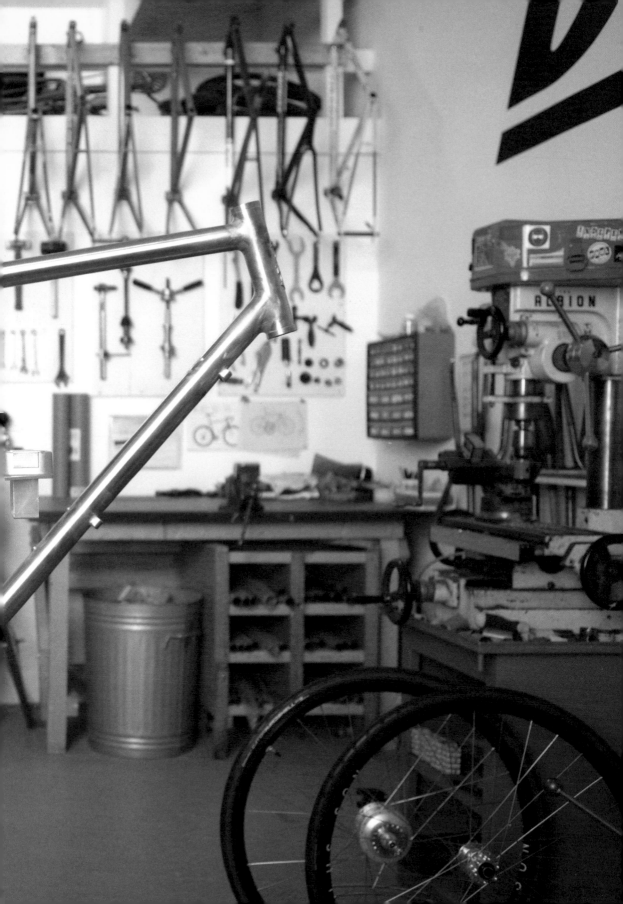

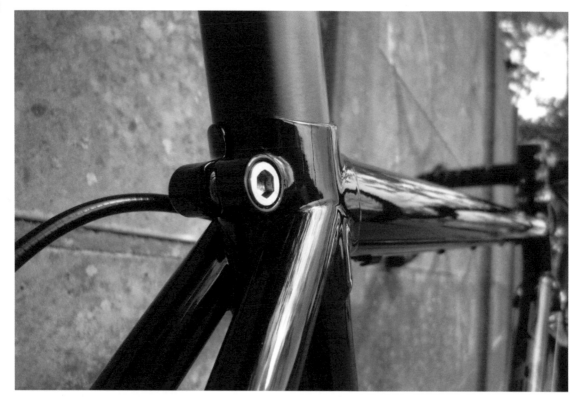

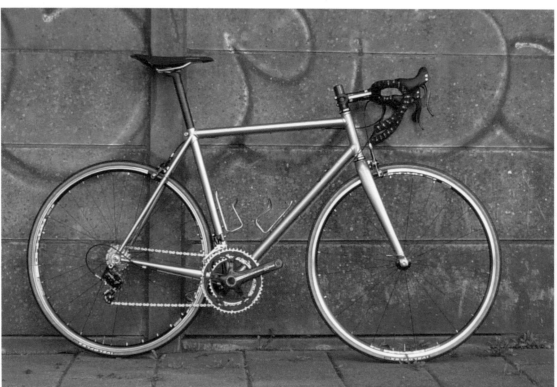

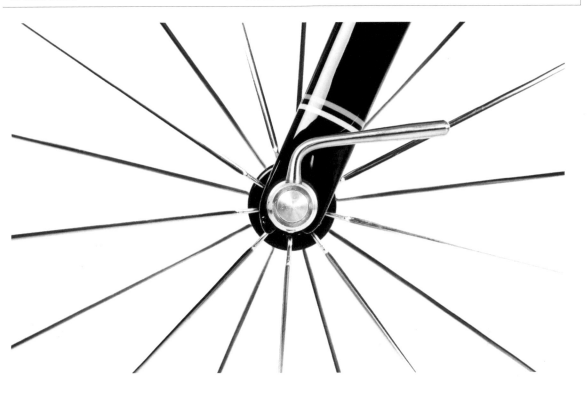

NDHOVEN, THE NETHERLANDS

ST JORIS CYCLES

"Your dream bike, it starts with a conversation on cycling over a cup of coffee", reads the company's website, and this statement summarises the whole process of buying a bike from St Joris Cycles.

St Joris specialises in the fusion of classic styles with contemporary materials, using high quality steel tubing that is equal parts light and strong. The company's focus is really on customer services and delivery while working with their client to produce a perfect, bespoke bicycle. Comprehensive fitting sessions to get the right size, working together on selecting materials and then components, and a detailed study of each client's anatomical characteristics all go into the design and production of each frame. Because of this, every bike is as individual and unique as its owner. St Joris even go for a ride with you when the bike is finished to make sure everything is working as it should be!

A testament to the quality and excellence of the bicycles produced at St Joris is their inclusion in the exclusive list of fine frame builders, cycle brand Rapha's *The Rapha Continental.*

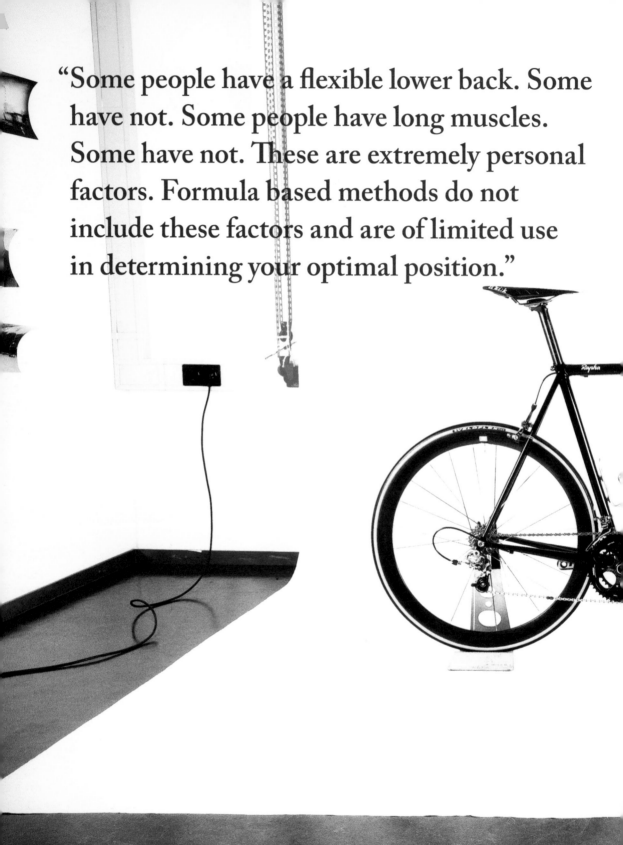

"Some people have a flexible lower back. Some have not. Some people have long muscles. Some have not. These are extremely personal factors. Formula based methods do not include these factors and are of limited use in determining your optimal position."

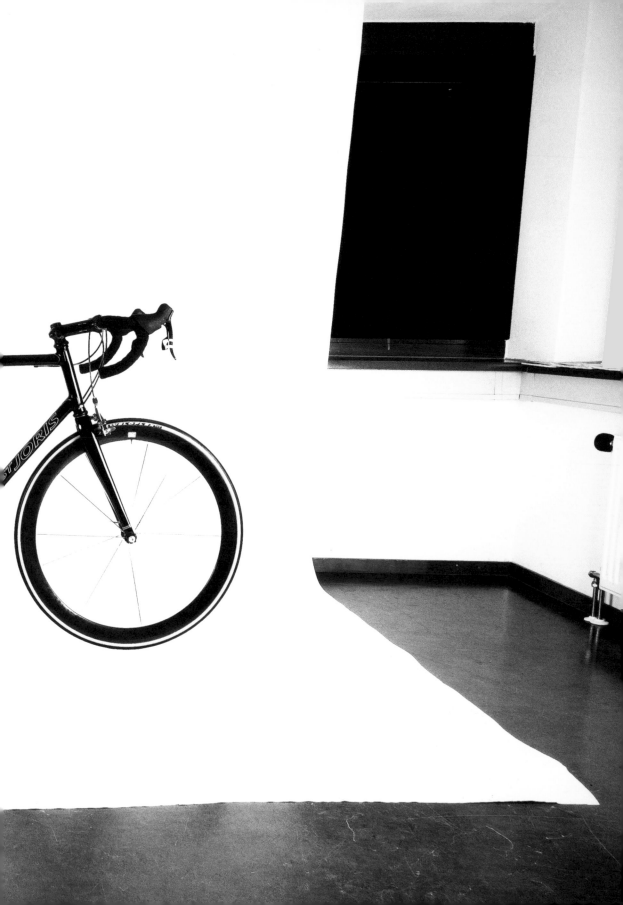

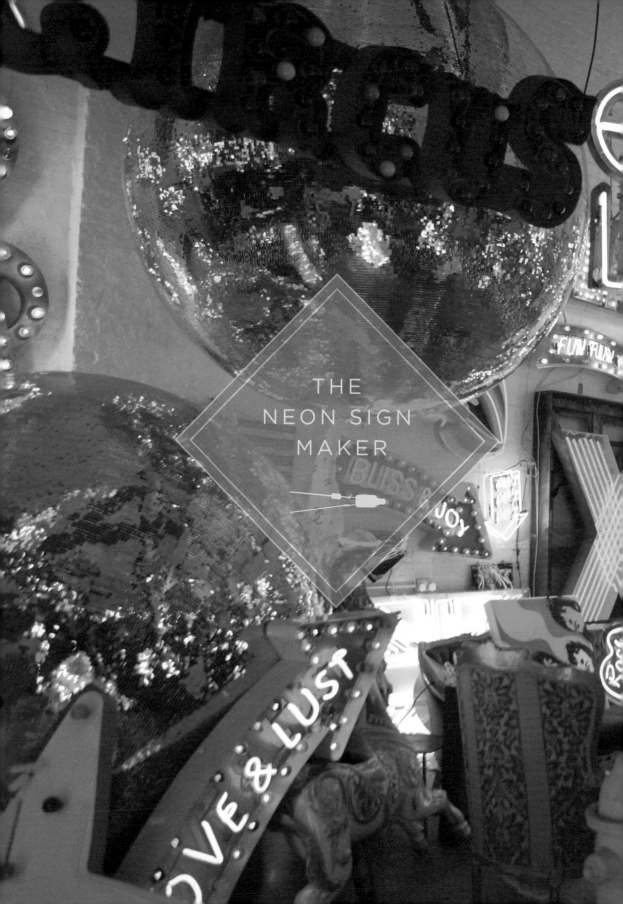

THE
NEON SIGN
MAKER

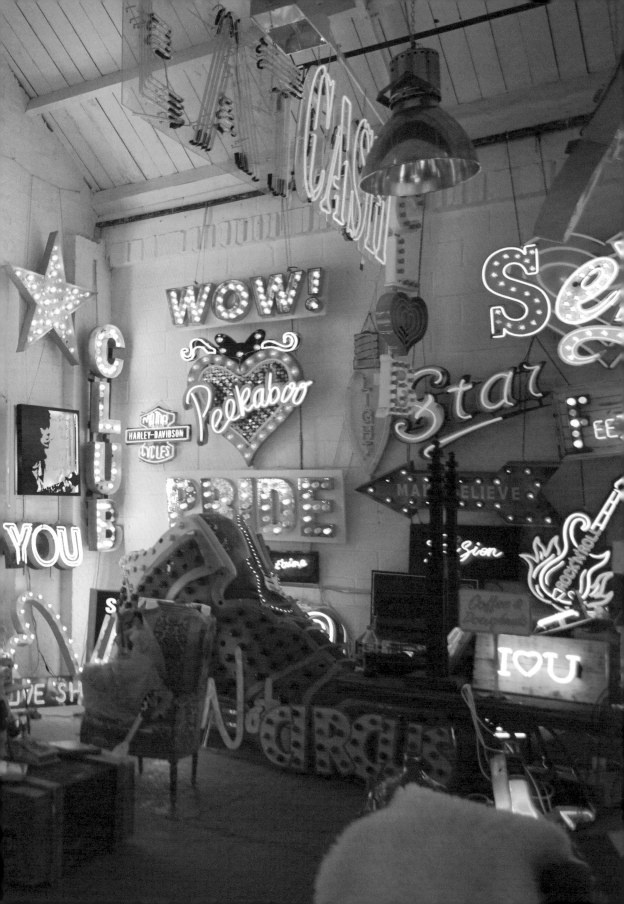

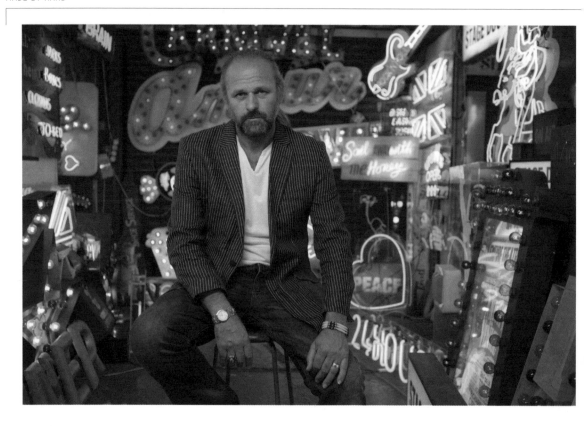

GOD'S OWN JUNKYARD

Chris Bracey is the United Kingdom's foremost neon sign maker. Having made his name in the 1960s as a graphic designer turned sign designer, Bracey was commissioned by many of Soho's infamous clubs to produce new signage and identities. His notoriety snowballed and now, years on, Bracey has made neon artworks for countless Hollywood films (*Eyes Wide Shut*, *Batman*, *Captain America* and *Charlie and The Chocolate Factory*, to name but a few) and numerous fashion houses including Vivian Westwood, Burberry and Mulberry.

Bracey's studio and showroom, titled God's Own Junkyard, has been something of an attraction since it opened, with day-trippers coming from far and wide to visit him in Walthamstow, London. The plight of the junkyard, subjected to a forced closure and relocation by property developers looking to redevelop the site, attracted a lot of media attention and community

sympathy, which fed into Bracey's high public profile. Now enjoying something of cult popularity both in London and Los Angeles (Los Angeles perhaps more so because of his work for cinema), he has recently moved premises to an even bigger showroom, four times the size of the original 'junkyard', and carrying the same name. The new junkyard, also in Walthamstow, contains a vast collection of Bracey's pieces, including his collaborative works with the likes of Martin Creed and David La Chappelle. It is, in fact, Europe's largest collection of neon signs.

He shares a lot of the industrious, resourceful and sustainable inclinations synonymous with the hand making community and as such is an avid recycler. Restoring vintage signage and 'upcycling' older pieces of neon or bulb work is as much a part of Bracey's passion as the production of new commissions.

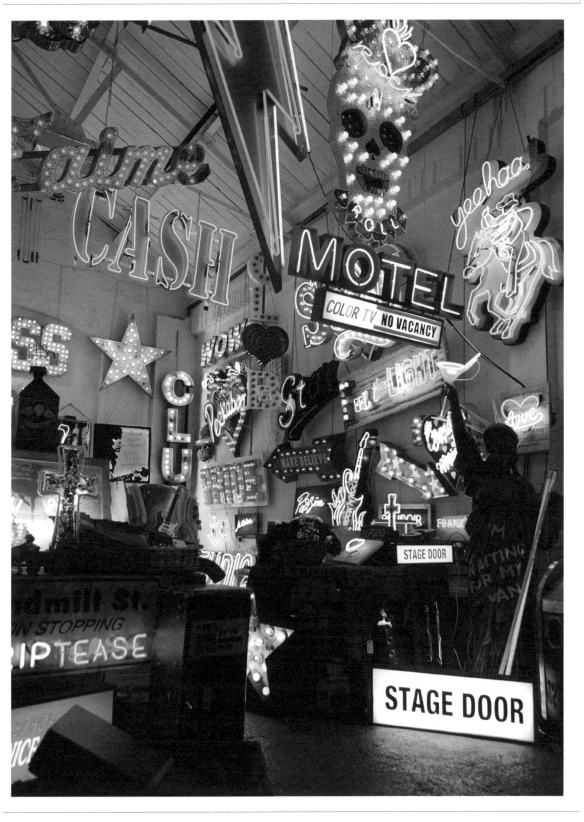

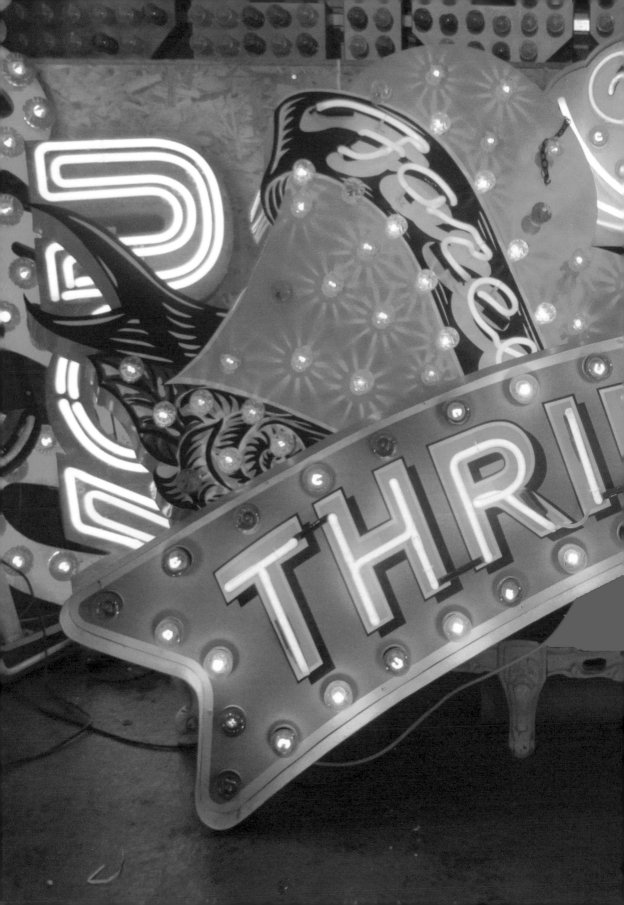

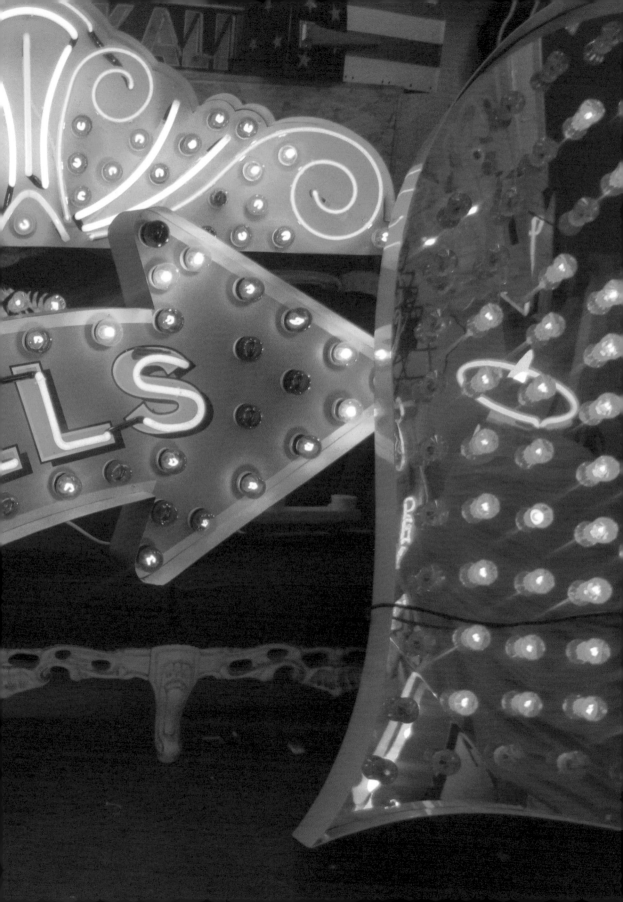

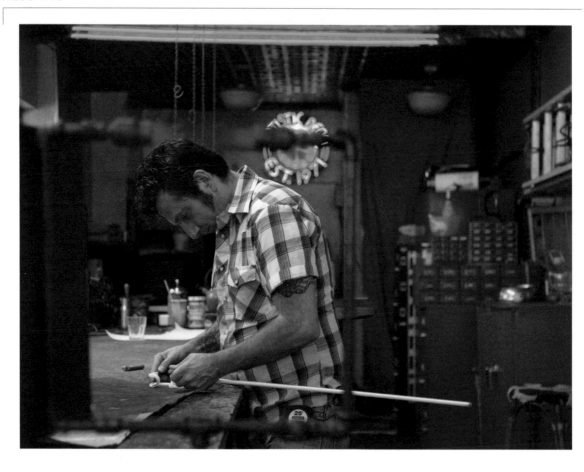

NEW YORK, UNITED STATES

ARTISTIC NEON

The history of Artistic Neon, Queens, New York, really goes back to 1952, when Gasper Ingui began learning the craft of neon. By 1971 when Ingui, now a talented and respected neon artist, opened his business Artistic Neon, the craft was seen by many as archaic and dying. He did everything he could to keep the craft alive, including taking commissions with many of New York's clubs and discos, and also teaching the neon craft at the Experimental Glass Workshop in New York for several years.

It was inevitable, really, that Ingui's son Robbie would be taught the trade, and now Robbie runs Artistic Neon and is, after 14 years of practice, a talented glass bender and neon designer. His passion for neon is evident in his reference to it as one of the few light sources that is still handmade, and talks at length about its efficiency, despite being over 100 years old it loses little energy.

Robbie bends glass tubing under heat, and then attaches electrodes to either end. The air is then sucked out using special tools, and neon or argon gas is pumped in. It is the gas that glows when electricity is introduced.

Robbie has had countless commissions around New York, favourites being the restoring of neon signs for 1950s Italian restaurants in the city—the proprietor of one of these restaurants once approached Robbie in tears as he was installing one of the restored signs, remembering the day when the original had been installed. "I like doing restorations because these signs have a long story to tell, and as the project evolves so does the story."

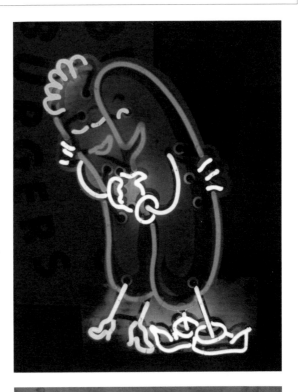

'I like to make art that, when you die, your kids will fight over.'

USTIN TEXAS, UNITED STATES

ROADSIDE RELICS

Todd Sanders is a pop artist through and through. His passion for commercial signage and the visual language of advertising shines through, quite literally, in his works of neon art. He has worked on both sides of this dichotomy, spending the first part of his career working for commercial sign writers, creating the signs that advertise products and companies to the passing trade, and the latter part focusing on his own artistic practice, which more critically appropriates the neon language.

Sanders started his neon journey as a graphic design student from Houston, Texas. A trip through Austin awoke his interest in neon and when he finished studying he relocated there and took up employment learning the craft of neon. After just three years he was operating his own commercial signage business, which he ran for over a decade before giving it up to focus exclusively on his art.

His work has featured on a Kings of Leon album cover (*Mechanical Bull*), in magazines including *Fortune* and *Esquire* and is now in the collections of celebrity clients including Willie Nelson, Shepard Fairey, Norah Jones, Johnny Depp and ZZ Top.

The name of his studio, Roadside Relics, comes from Sanders' passion for the neon culture of the roadsides of the south-central United States. Used to glowingly advertise cafes, diners and gas stations, these vintage neon signs inspired the maker's practice to the extent that he has developed processes to accelerate rust in the production of these faux-vintage neon pieces, viewing the aging of a piece of neon as part of its beauty, as much as the neon and argon's iridescent shimmer.

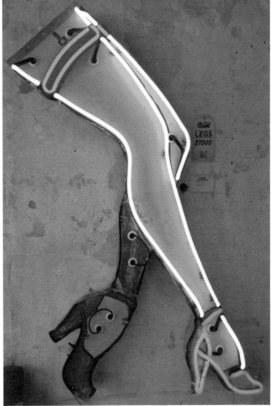

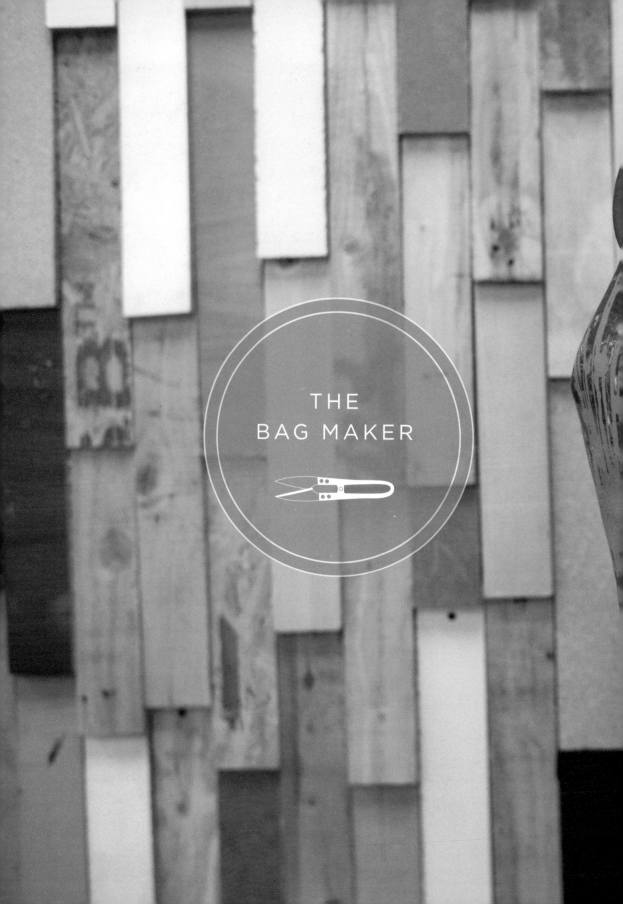

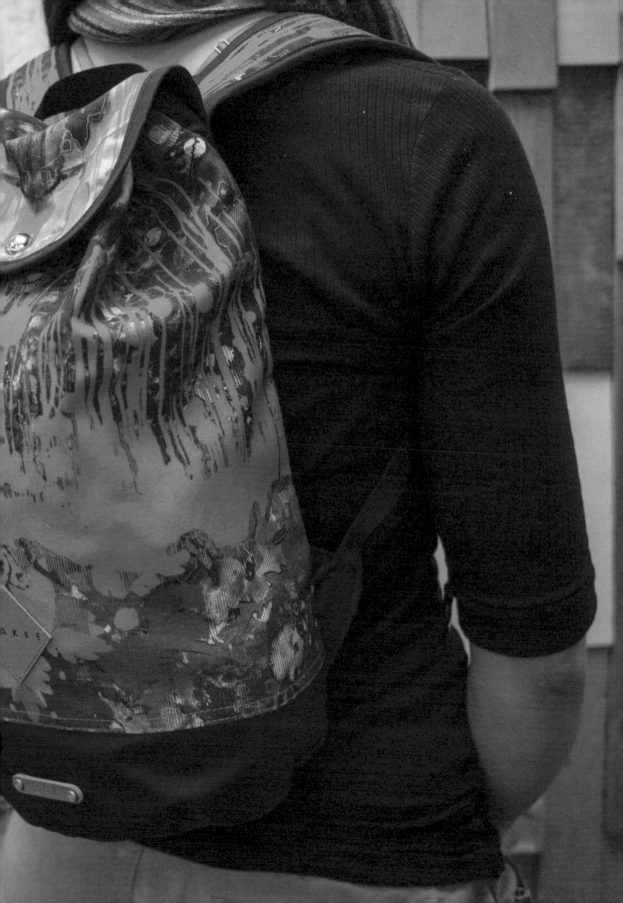

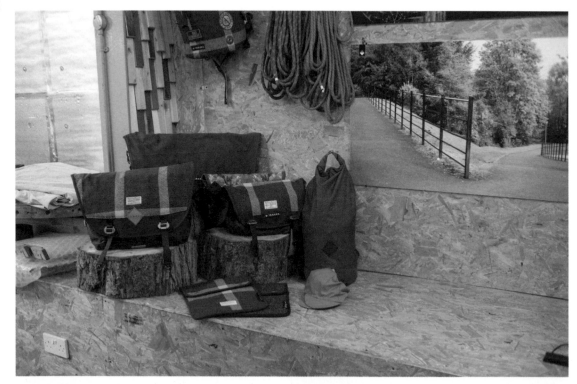

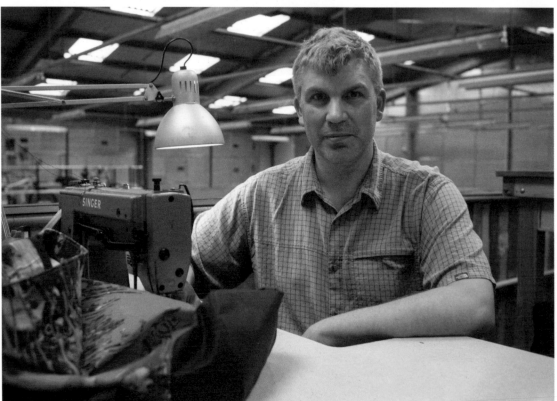

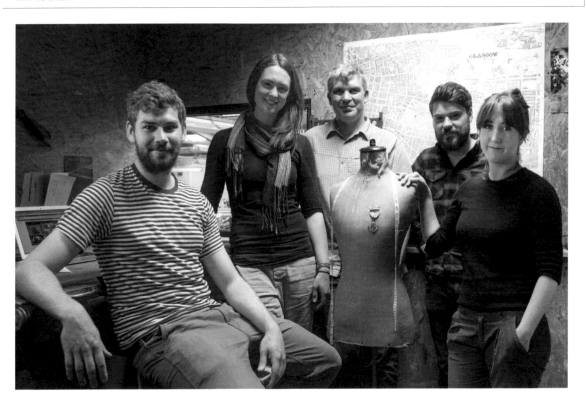

GLASGOW, UNITED KINGDOM

TRAKKE BAGS

When Alec Farmer was studying Visual Communication and Graphic Design at Glasgow School of Art, he and his friends, fulfilling the stereotype of broke students, would rummage through skips looking for useful materials for their work, pulling out old canvas banners, pieces of sofas and suitcases. These materials, combined with a passion for cycling, were the foundations for Glasgow-based bag company Trakke.

Farmer and a friend started making courier-style bags for themselves and their cyclist buddies using these abandoned materials, following no pattern and taking design only from what was available to them at the time. Today, the Trakke team works out of a small warehouse space making several different models of bags for cyclists, but also adventurers, commuters and anyone else! A pattern cutter, a couple of machinists, someone to check the finish—these are the only sets of hands a Trakke bag passes through during production.

Placing importance upon local manufacture, Trakke's production site and offices are in immediate proximity to each other, meaning that the development of their bags is a constant back-and-forth between maker and user. Their warehouse factory is also in the same building as Glasgow Bike Station so constant feedback and testing by the Glasgow cycling community means Trakke bags are constantly improving.

While other outdoor pursuits companies place emphasis on 'performance' and 'technology', using lightweight, breathable and water repellent synthetics, Trakke follow the 'heritage' line. They use traditional and durable materials that age well and maintain their functionality over a long life span. Trakke have two main ranges of bags, one based on their ongoing collaboration with Hebrides-made Harris Tweed and the other using waxed cotton. Trakke's use of these materials, along with their use of metal components made in Wales and webbing for straps made in Derbyshire are testament to the company's wish to keep supply local.

"We live in a disposable society. Back in the day, manufacturers would build products to last. They were a serious investment. We think that they had the right idea!"

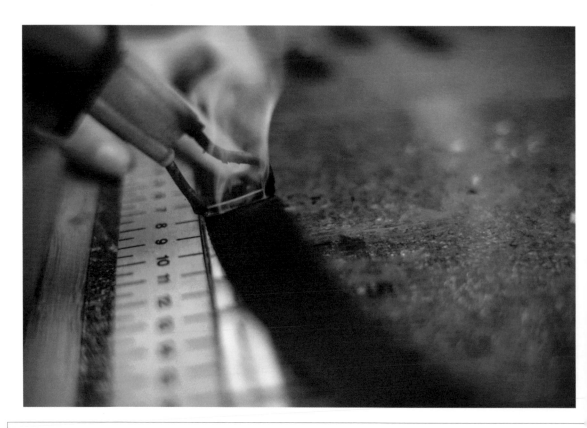

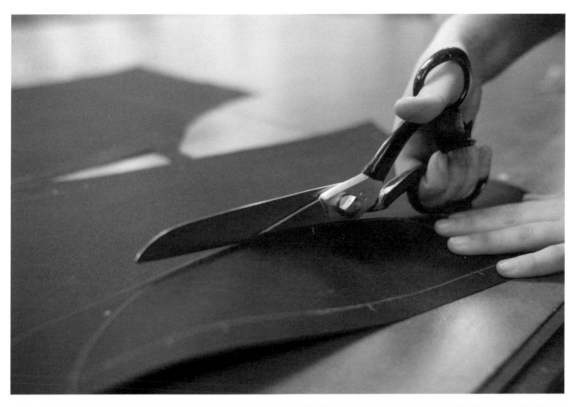

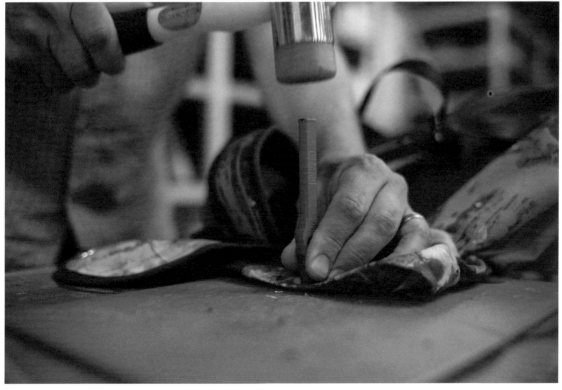

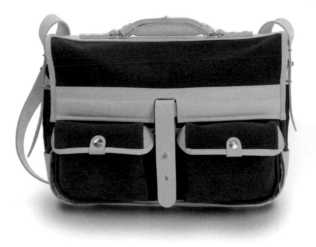

SAN FRANCISCO, UNITED STATES

JOHN CHO MOORE

John Cho Moore makes high-quality one-off briefcases and backpacks in a practice that centres around belief in craft, design and bridging cultures. Unquestionably influenced by a history in design—he spent some time after graduating from the Rhode Island School of Design in corporate product design, during which he felt uncomfortably aware of the disposable nature of the products he was designing and the disconnected, hands-off quality of the process—he combines his skills in design with personal creation.

As a contemporary craftsman, Moore is a protagonist for combining state of the art technologies with traditional craft, and the symbiotic relationship that can develop between the two. While he passionately believes in the lessons we can learn from time-honoured, dedicated techniques, he sees equal importance in incorporating these with modern methods and resources. Tools available to the modern craftsman mean making is more exciting and accessible than ever before; without advanced appliances, cheap high-quality cameras and online market places, for example, the practice could not exist in the

form it does. As he puts it, his products are "the result of taking the best tools, ideas, production methods and inspiration from both the past as well as the present". Plus, by making the two inseparable not only is the best of both worlds available, using 'apprentice based trades' within modern production goes some way toward their preservation in present-day life.

And this two-way relationship is reflected in the fact that, born to Japanese parents in the United States, and raised between the two countries, Moore has garnered inspiration from two countries, which contribute equally, though diversely, to his final practice. San Francisco, an area he describes as going through a "local manufacturing renaissance", is a supporting and inspirational "DIY start up" community for hand makers and the modern-day craftsman. Kyoto, Japan, is home to the culture of devoted craft which first inspired Moore to make, and where he sources a key material for his designs: bamboo, provided by a fourth generation family-run specialist business.

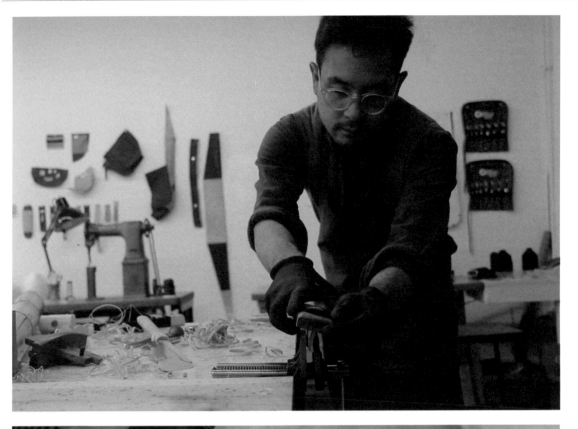

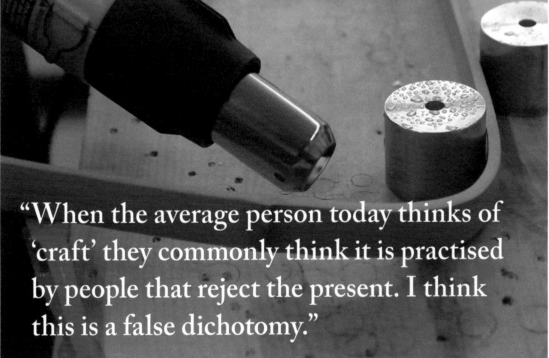

"When the average person today thinks of 'craft' they commonly think it is practised by people that reject the present. I think this is a false dichotomy."

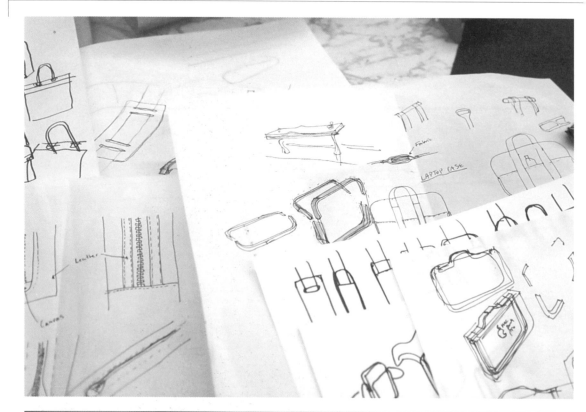

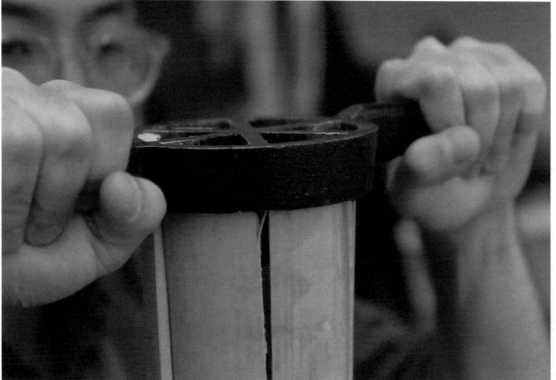

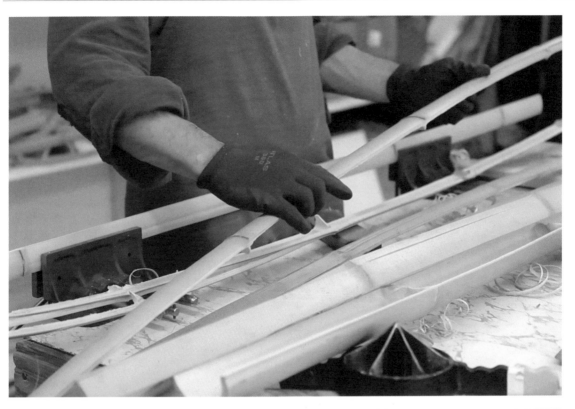

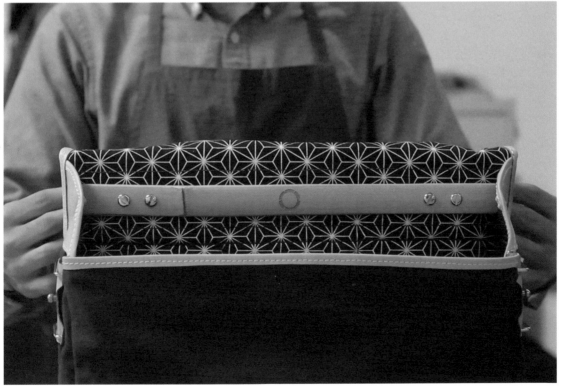

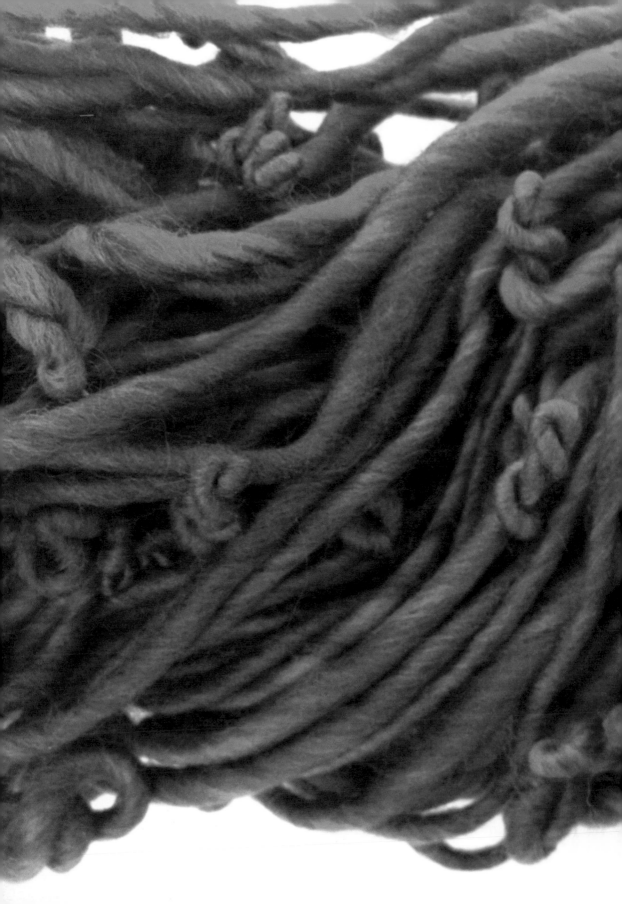

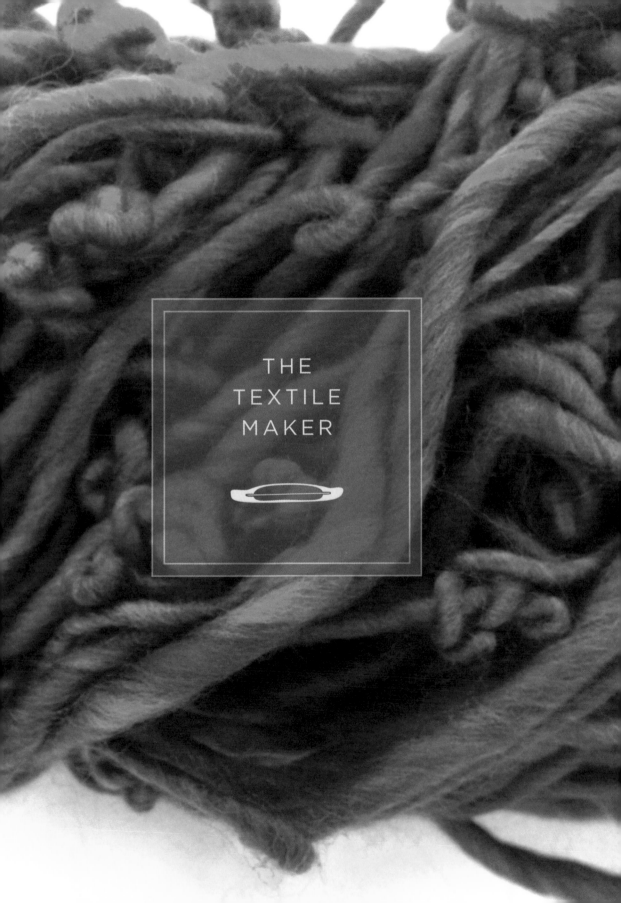

THE
TEXTILE
MAKER

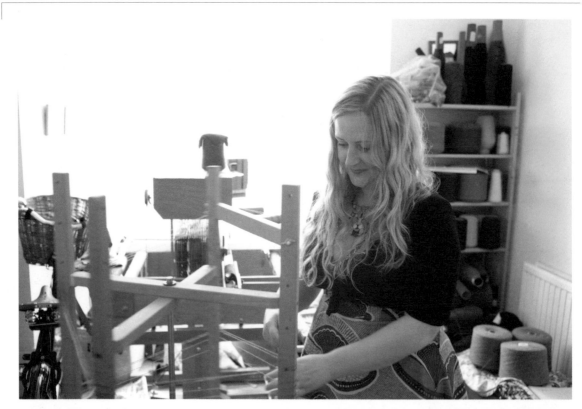

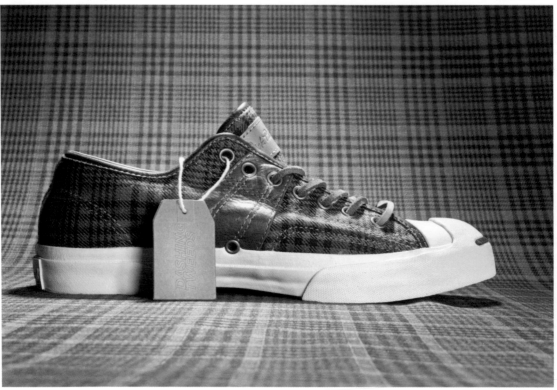

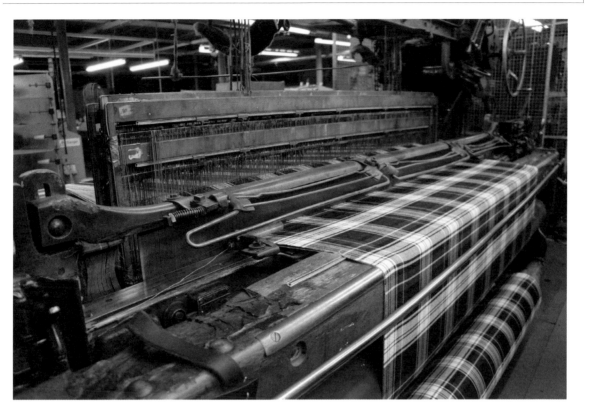

ONDON, UNITED KINGDOM

DASHING TWEEDS

Inspired by discontinued tweeds found in the archives of Savile Row tailors, fashion photographer Guy Hills commissioned the woven textile designer, and Royal College of Art graduate, Kirsty McDougall, to create a one-off design. So successful was their first endeavour that they set up their own weave design studio. Now with a shop in London's tailoring district, a number of design collaborations, and a 'ready to wear' collection of their own, Dashing Tweeds are helping to bring contemporary woven wools to public attention.

Hills explains that within the definition of tweed ("colourful woven wool with twill structure") there is room for variation, and creating their own has allowed Dashing Tweeds to play with the outcomes much more liberally. They now have 50 fabric designs of their own—a collection comprising both handmade fabrics and those made with powered looms, all specially woven with dyed fibres (all in all, a process that can take up to a month to finish).

And, while they cater for the dandier customer or tailor, Hills also places emphasis upon growing public interest in tweed; a current fascination, with the material, and modern incarnations like those made by Dashing Tweeds, keeping mills, and the various skills needed to weave, alive.

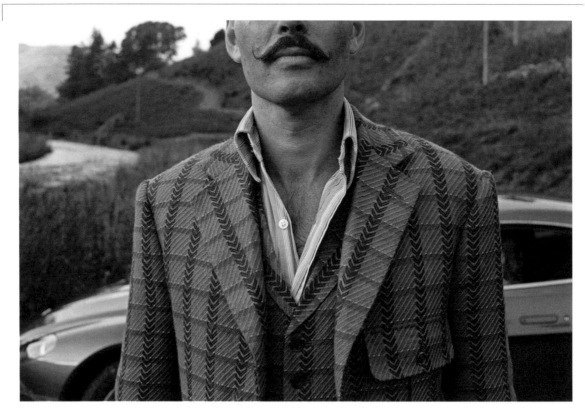

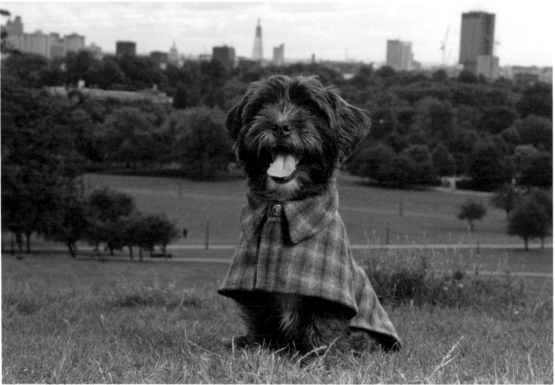

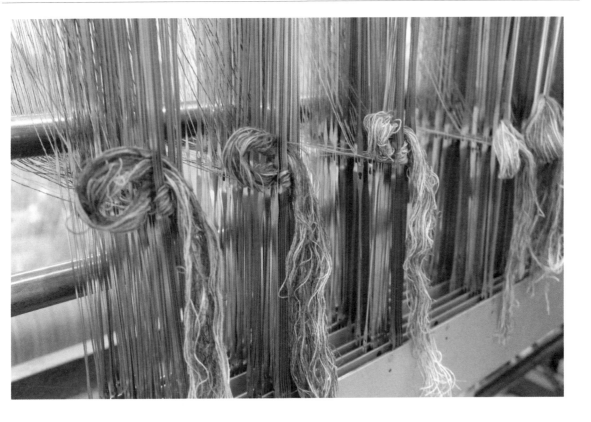

"In an age of machine mass-production, the love that is imparted into something when it is handmade is what now creates desirability."

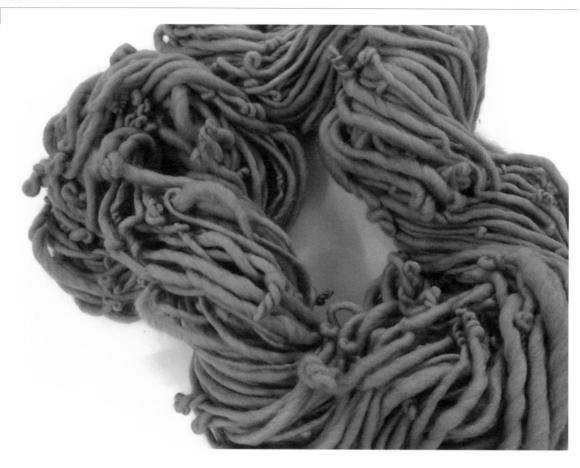

LONDON, UNITED KINGDOM

SHEEP OF STEEL

The age-old craft of yarn spinning is made twenty-first century in the design consciously eye-catching and thought-provoking hand-spun yarns of London-based Sheep of Steel. The project of Irem Arig—literally, it was a result of the Central St Martins graduate's final degree project, for which she dyed, blended and spun her own yarn—Sheep of Steel's forte is spinning creative yarns from innovative materials including textile waste and sustainable plant fibres.

Giving free rein to a naturally experimental approach to design, and fuelled by curiosity, Irem started her spinning career playing with every wool, plant and animal fibre she could get hold of, a phase in which she discovered the options opened up by making by hand. Hand spinning, in comparison to faster contemporary machine-operated alternatives, allows for more manipulation of the materials and thus a broader scope of creative results: texture from tucking in morsels of cocoon strippings or recycled plastic fibres, or bobbling by deliberate over twisting, for example.

Now, Sheep of Steel doesn't only create their own yarns, but also works in collaboration with clients and other designers on specialist commissioned projects.

"I recognised early on that by hand spinning a yarn, you are able to play around with certain materials and techniques, which the machinery in spinning mills are incapable of doing."

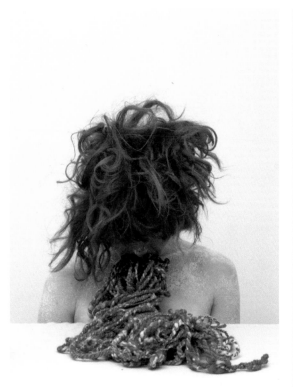

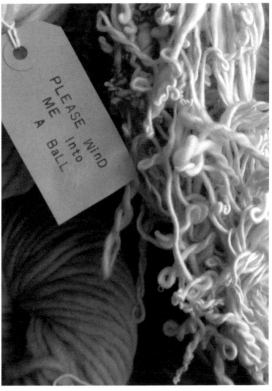

"These unusual effects can only be achieved by the hand of man!"

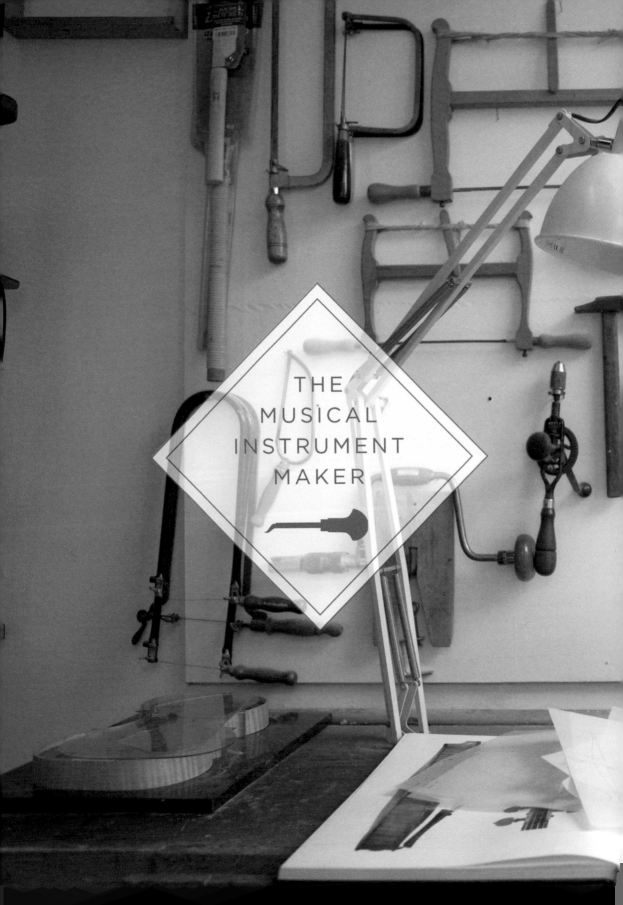

THE
MUSICAL
INSTRUMENT
MAKER

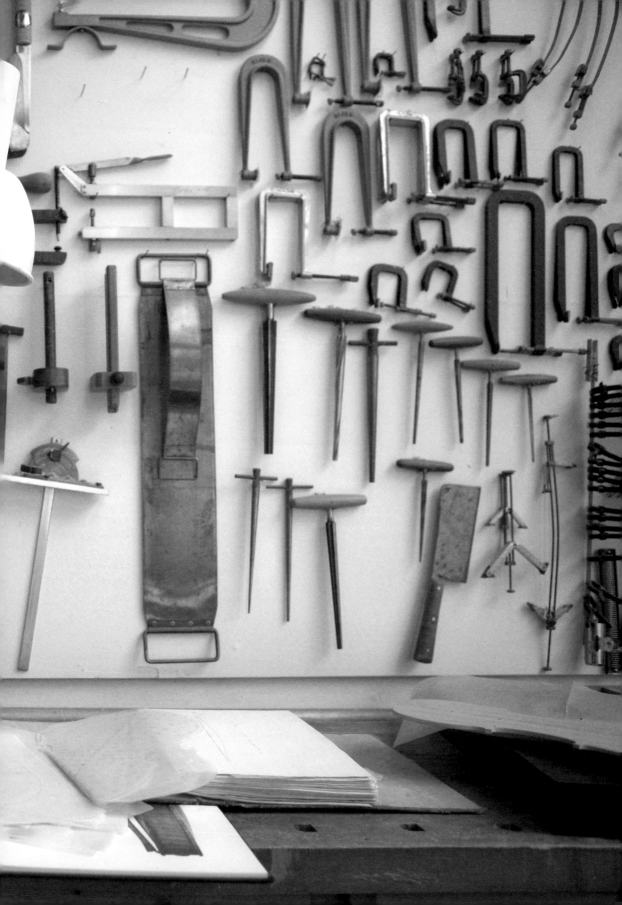

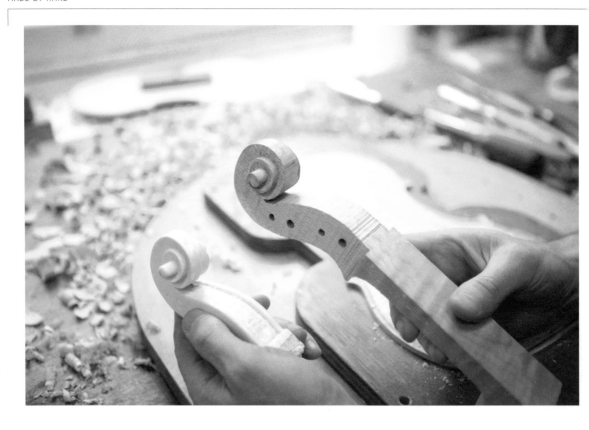

ANDREAS HUDELMAYER

Andreas Hudelmayer works out of a small workshop in Clerkenwell, London. The workshop, conveniently close to classical music hotspots such as the Barbican and London Symphony Orchestra's St Luke's, is an Aladdin's cave of violin-making components and tools. The small footprint of the workshop and its high ceilings mean that Hudelmayer's various ephemera have spread up the walls in racks and shelves, giving the space a busy, crowded yet perfectly functional feeling.

Hudelmayer has wanted to be a violin maker since he was a teenager. He had a love for music, inherited from his parents and family, and a love of craft and woodworking, so it seemed like an ideal path. Leaving his native South Germany and moving to the United Kingdom to study at the Newark School of Violin Making, where he passed with distinction. After working some years back in Germany, at a Berlin-based violin makers, he became the workshop manager at Frederick Phelps in London, where he spent five years working closely with a variety of clients.

Since 2002 Hudelmayer has been working independently, making violins for respected, high-profile musicians including Raphael Wallfisch, Igor Ozim, Gordan Nikolitch, Howard Davis, David Fruehwirth and Henrik Hochschild. Each violin takes around two months to construct and involves fine wood working using chisels, planes and picks, as well as the use of sound recording and tuning equipment in order to achieve an exact sound.

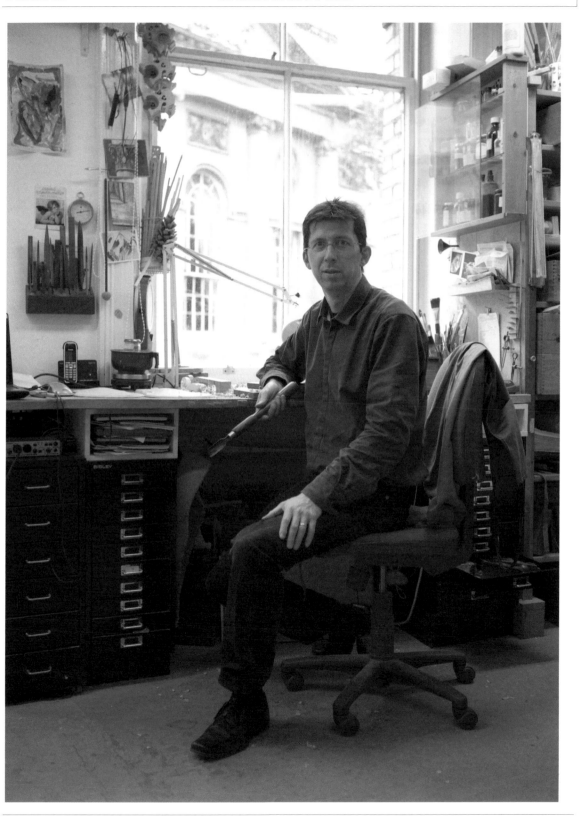

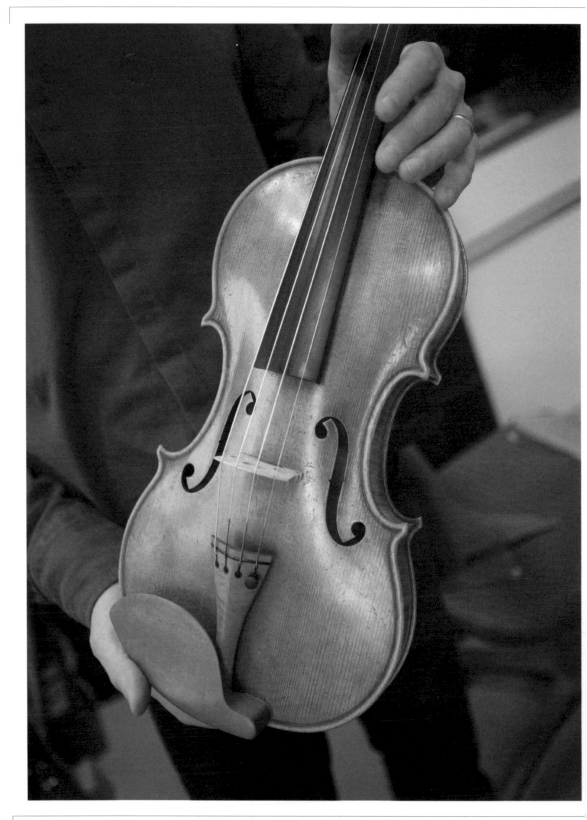

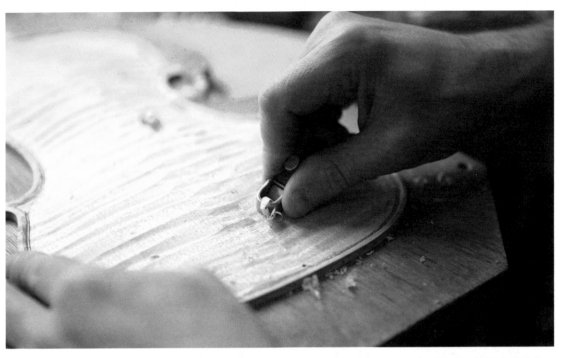

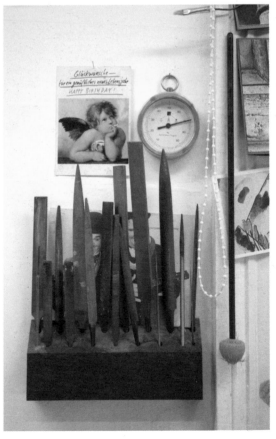

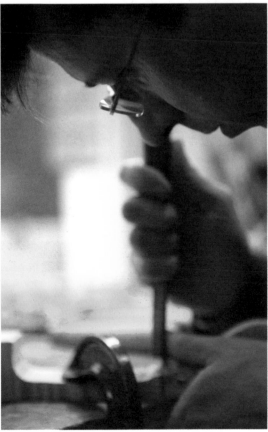

"Opening my own studio was the culmination of a dream I first had in a dull history lesson as a teenager. Back then, I thought violin making would be the perfect combination of my interests: music, engineering and woodwork. 20 years on, I can't imagine doing anything else."

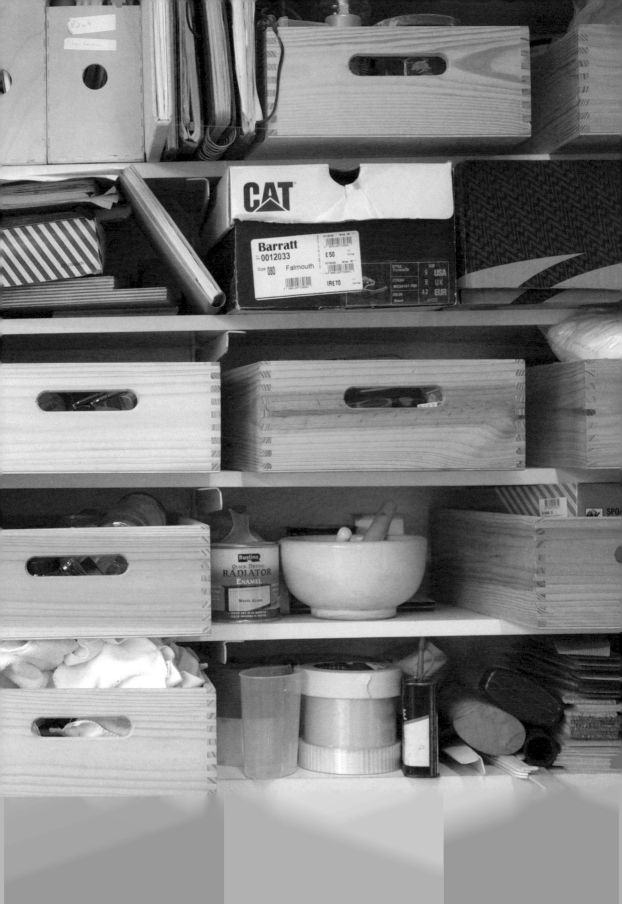

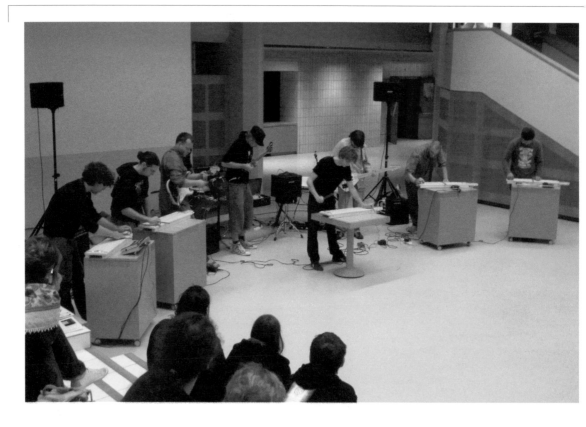

AMSTERDAM, THE NETHERLANDS

YURI LANDMAN

As a child, the radical luthier Yuri Landman suffered from fever dreams, during which he experienced sensory distortion including humming drones and high pitches, sounds he later heard approximated in the avant-garde no-wave work of Glenn Branca and Sonic Youth. His interest in sonic experimentation was initially piqued via those artists' use of prepared guitar—"... when you place objects on the knotted harmonic overtone positions of a string, you get the most incredible beautiful overtones resonating on top of some lower fundamental tones"— though it was a bandmate's encounter with Bradford Reed and his Pencilina zither on the streets of New York that inspired him to start creating his own instruments. "This ambition", he states, "evolved, and became my current job: an inventor of musical instruments."

Landman utilises basic materials in his constructions —originally collecting found wood and disassembling electronic devices to collect their bolts, screws, nuts and inner mechanics "in the tradition of the Arte Povera movement... born out of need as I was rather poor at the time", and now favouring cheap DIY-store soft woods and other appropriated objects such as pre-fab steel, harpsichord string and PET soda bottles—forgoing slick aesthetics for pure functionality, and following the idiosyncratic remit that whatever he builds must fit in a suitcase: "Designing a portable version of a good sounding concept is the most difficult part of the process. Dinosaurs died out because they were too big."

The importance of the 'handmade' aspect of Landman's practice is implicit in the idiosyncrasies of his designs, though he is explicit about its benefits:

"It's a convenient method to come to new sound results you won't easily achieve with mass manufactured stuff. It's not a holy rule that everybody should follow, but it works very well for me, as well as a musicians like Hans Reichel, Z'EV, Pierre Bastien, Thomas Truax, Neptune. We feel more liberated in our own gear."

RUCCI

Michael Rucci's interest in creating homemade oscillatory synthesisers, drone boxes and analogue modulators and mixers began as a child, initially in simply taking things apart, before graduating to making simple modifications and repairs on musical equipment, and then taking a basic electronics course as part of a recording engineering program. He began building his own oscillators and other units in 2008—"[It's] hard to say what drove me to this at first; I tend to be quick to try new things. This just happened to really consume me from the beginning."

The instruments Rucci now produces and sells take the form of super-stripped-back multi-dial micro-units, produced largely with salvaged wood and metal—sourced via rubbish sites and Bay Area thrift shops—but also discarded and repurposed jars, video game controllers, toys and the housings of obsolete electronics, though he adds that he does occasionally seek specific materials depending on his conceptual ideas. The resulting units produce a sound as equivalently "handmade" as their aesthetic, minimal and raw. This, for Rucci—and doubtless the analogue enthusiasts who are drawn to his work—is key to their appeal: "The controls simply make them more of an instrument than a piece of equipment. For the most part there are no mass-produced alternatives with the same combination of simplicity and raw sound. I think that the people who are drawn to these types of instruments appreciate what others may see as a limitation."

Fundamentally, Rucci's practice is also based on a desire to create things with longevity, objects that can survive 'disposable' culture, believing that people are too swift to trash and replace their affects: "When everything is built on such a large scale", he states, "nothing is special —everything is replaceable."

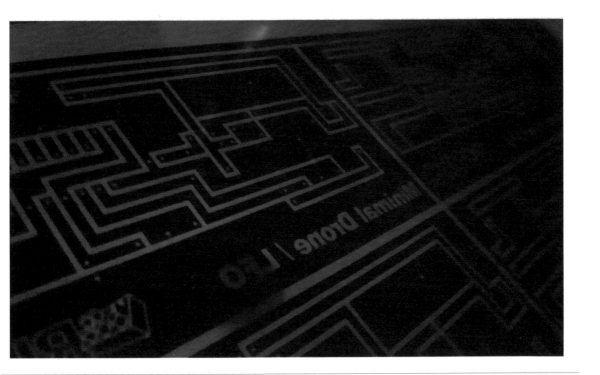

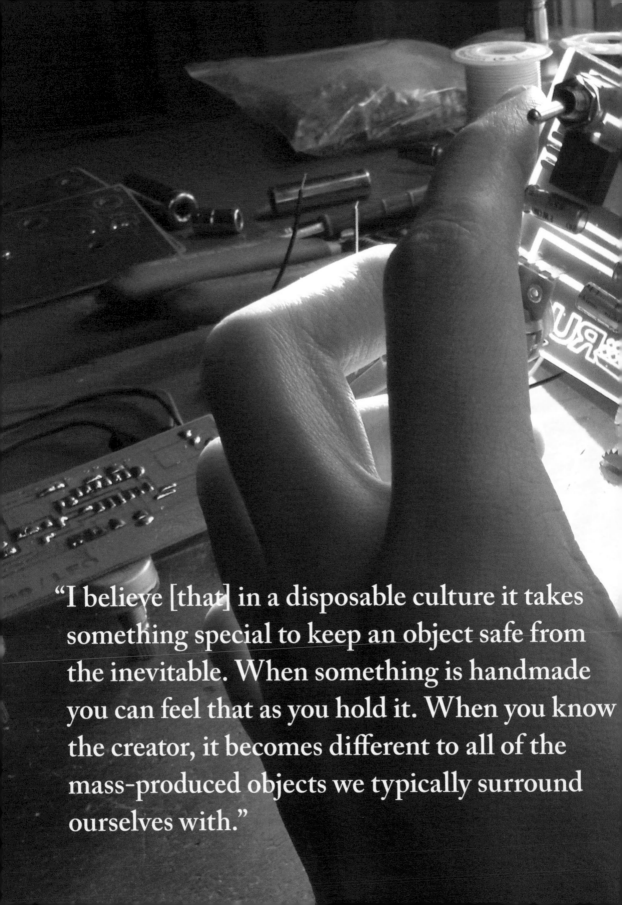

"I believe [that] in a disposable culture it takes something special to keep an object safe from the inevitable. When something is handmade you can feel that as you hold it. When you know the creator, it becomes different to all of the mass-produced objects we typically surround ourselves with."

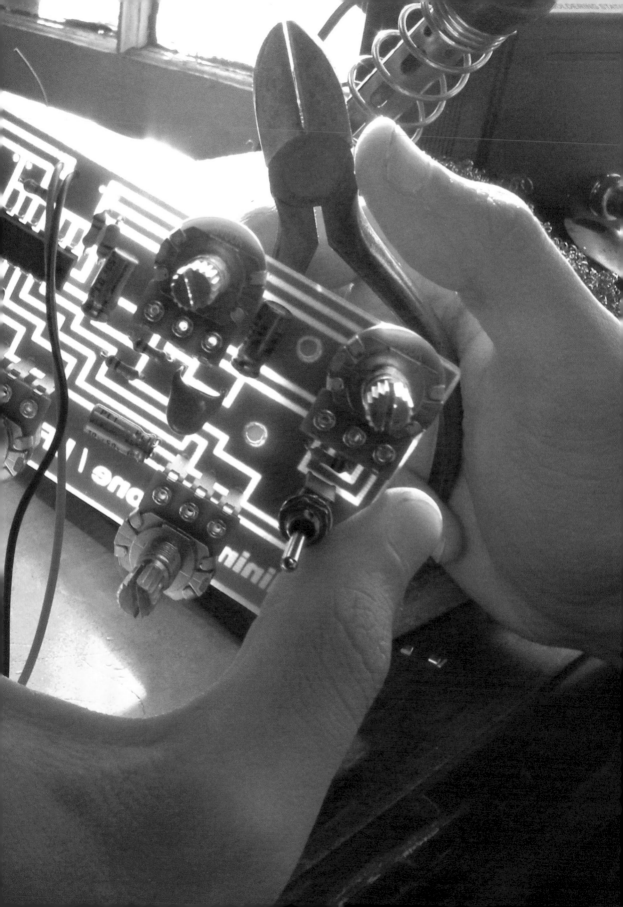

THE
GLASSWORKER

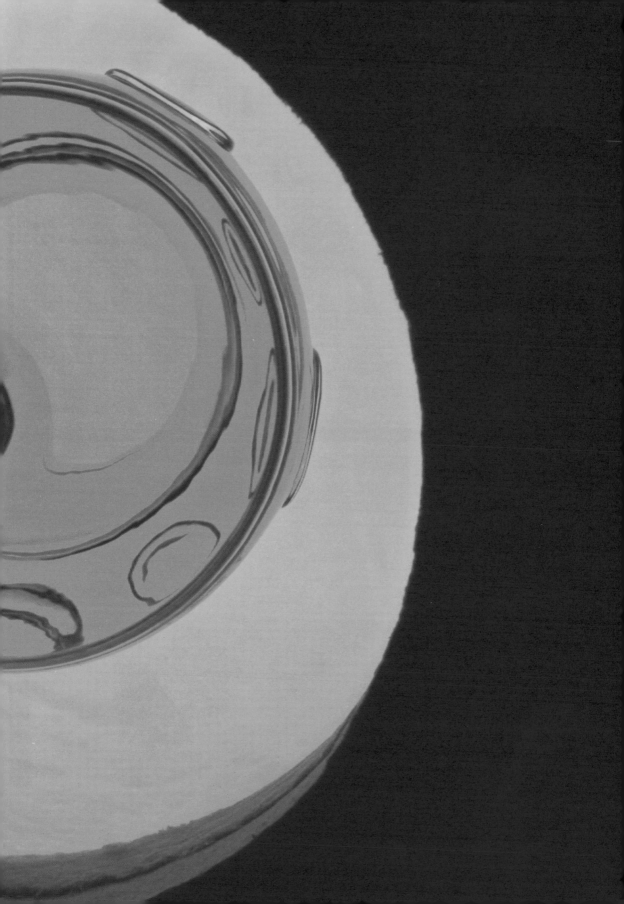

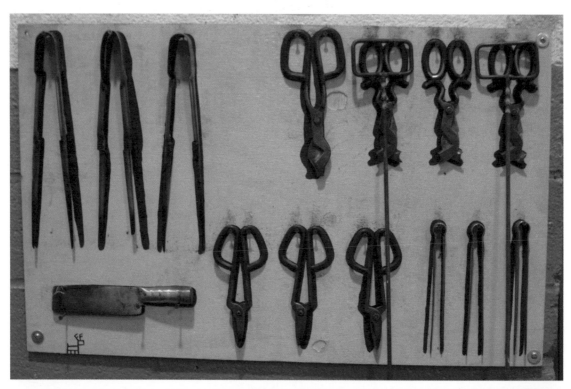

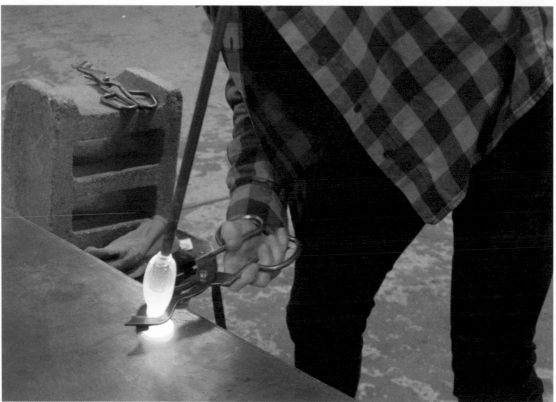

BROOKLYN GLASS

Glass blowing as a practice has been around since sometime BC, depending on your source, making it one of the oldest crafts to be featured in this book. In the modern metropolis, though, where glassware is predominantly machine-blown and mass-produced, such a craft is all but forgotten. Or at least, that was the situation in New York only a few years ago, until 2011, when Alan Iwamura, David Ablon and Kat Ablon founded Brooklyn Glass. At the time there was no comparable operation anywhere in New York's five boroughs.

As well as producing their own designs in contemporary glassware, both ornamental and functional, every single one ultimately unique, Brooklyn Glass have open studios for other practitioners to use in their glass blowing and production of neon/cold cathode and lamp working. Additionally, the organisation also welcomes newcomers on courses and workshops, to learn the skills needed to recreationally or professionally pursue glass blowing.

The emphasis at Brooklyn Glass is on craft and skill itself, and on preserving the knowledge base of glass blowing by repopulating the world with educated blowers, whilst also providing facilities for already skilled craftspeople to work in. The organisation is a pertinent example of the close knit community and locally minded inclination of hand makers worldwide, especially in the epicentres of craft such as Brooklyn, where new hand making businesses are springing up constantly. The founding members became aware that Brooklyn had more and more people interested in working with glass who had neither the skills nor resources to do so. This was coupled with a growing desire by consumers to support local business and reject global import— an unsustainable and economically unviable means of consumption.

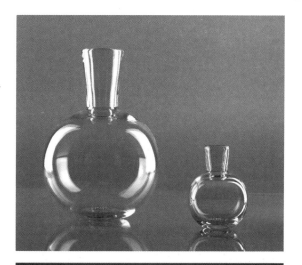

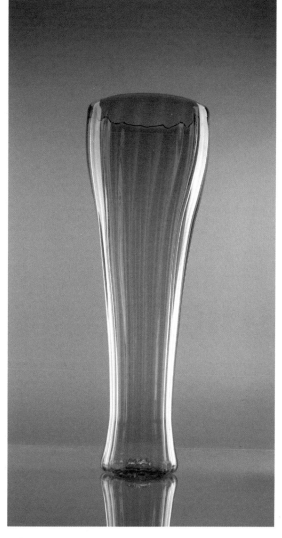

"No handmade piece of glass is ever exactly the same, making every object individual and unique. Today historical processes have merged with contemporary ideas and designs, generating new breadth and depth within the creative processes of glass makers."

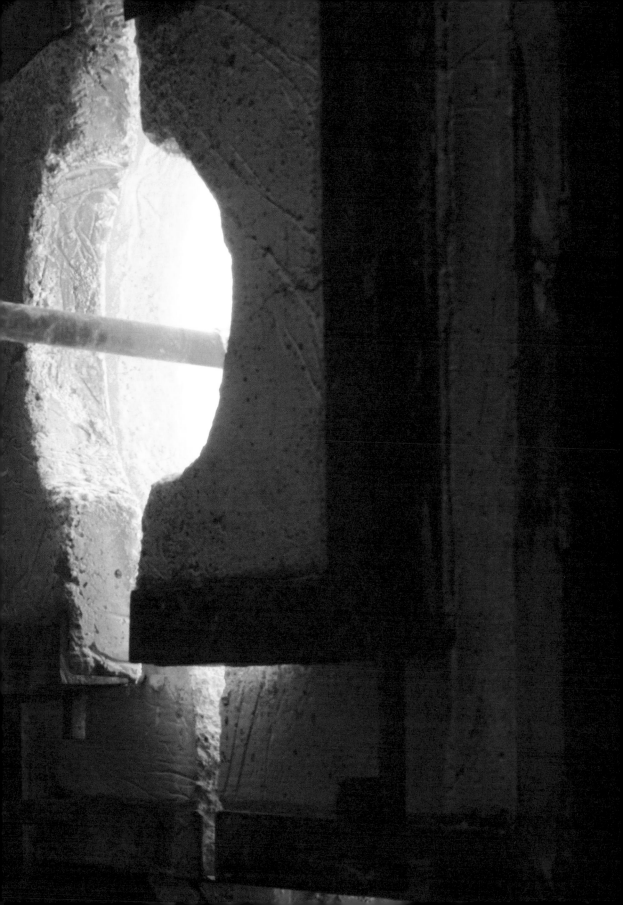

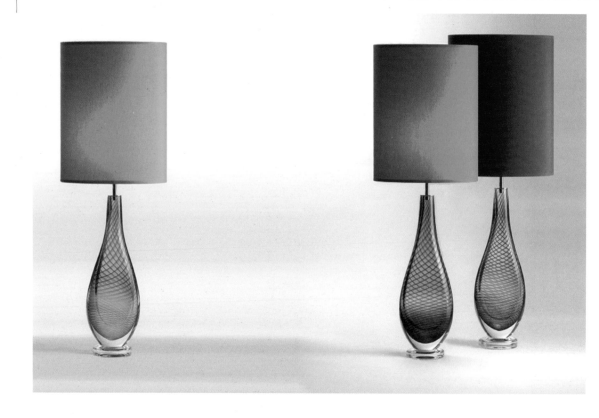

CHATTERIS, UNITED KINGDOM

STEWART HEARN

Stewart Hearn produces unique pieces of glassware for exhibitions and high-end retailers such as Fortnum & Mason, The Conran Shop and Heal's. His craft, something he studied at college and has now been practising for over 30 years, is an ancient one, and one that in many ways has not changed in hundreds of years. The basis fundamentals, the heating of sand to make glass, and the rotation and blowing through pipes in order to shape the molten glass, remain the same. The materials used, however, are infinitely more advanced, and the role that technology plays in the workshop means that now the laborious and inefficient elements of the process have been taken care of, allowing the very skilled tasks of the actual blowing, shaping and cutting to occupy the blower's focus.

Hearn's use of colour and clean lines resonate with clients who are looking for a bespoke handmade technique for their own designs. A large part of his ability to draw in work from contemporary designers is his willingness to work side-by-side with them in prototyping sessions. By allowing designers to work collaboratively with the material and the maker, Hearn educates them in the qualities of glass and the process of blowing so that the craft becomes the starting point in the design process and not an after thought.

When asked why this way of working is so important, Hearn mentions how so many techniques have already been lost and talks of the importance in skills being passed on properly. He sees it as his duty to keep techniques alive, and to try to create new ones. Hearn feels that he is always "striving to be as good as previous masters and, of course, to be better too", he remarks; "It's something that not everybody has a chance to do and the fact that we're allowed to play with fire everyday, it's quite special."

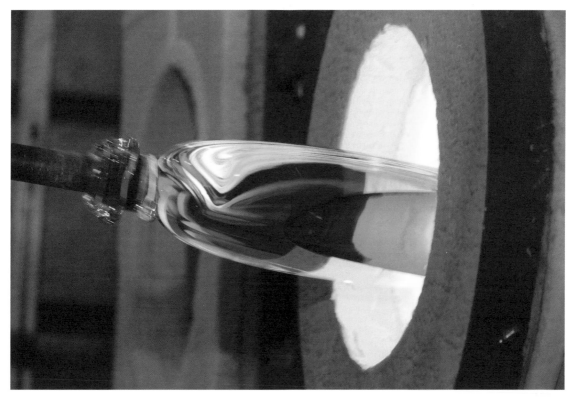

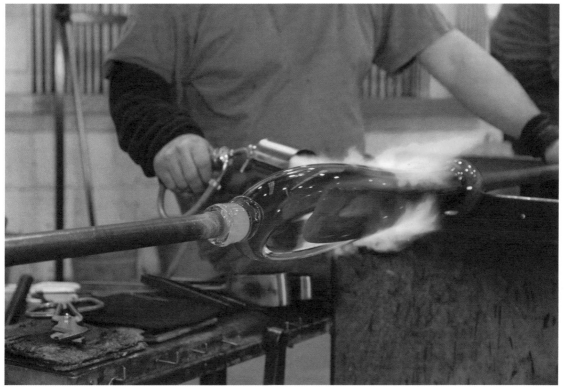

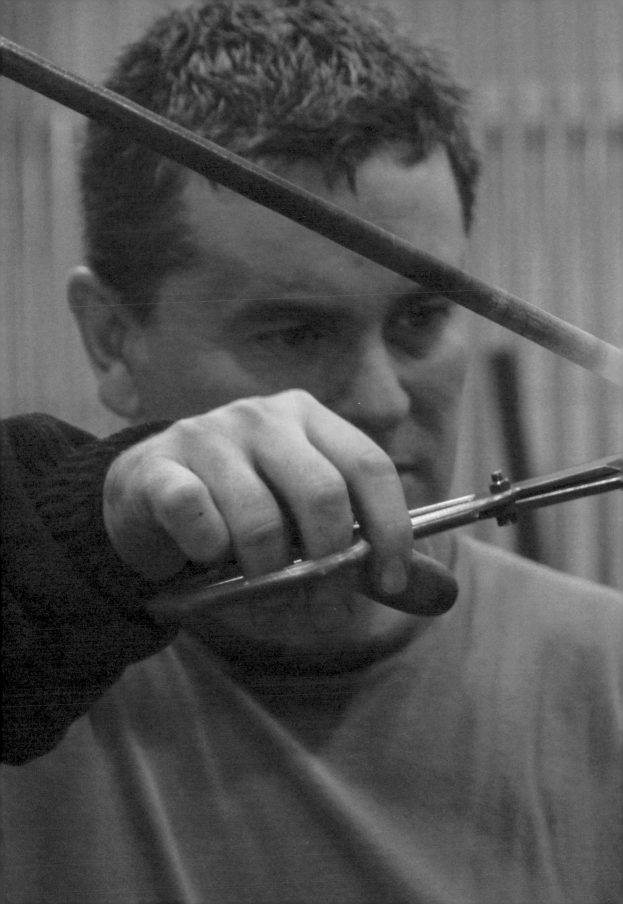

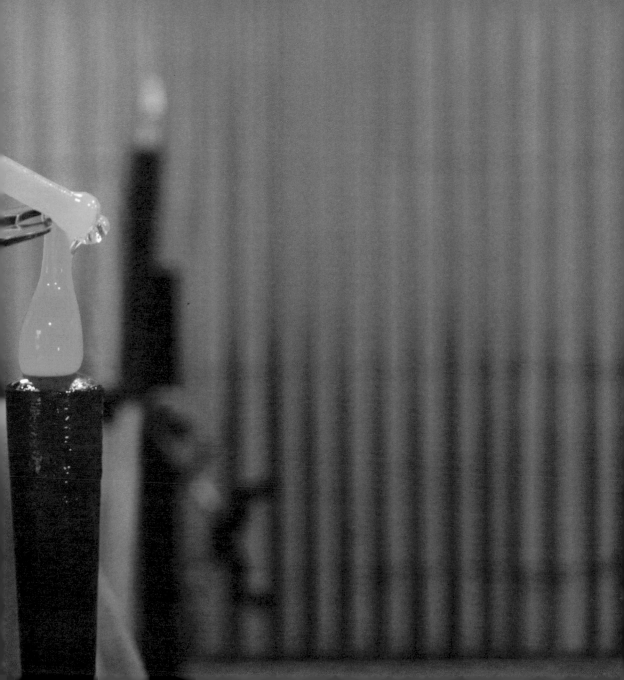

"I always joke that my wife commutes to work in London while I get to play with fire in the garden."

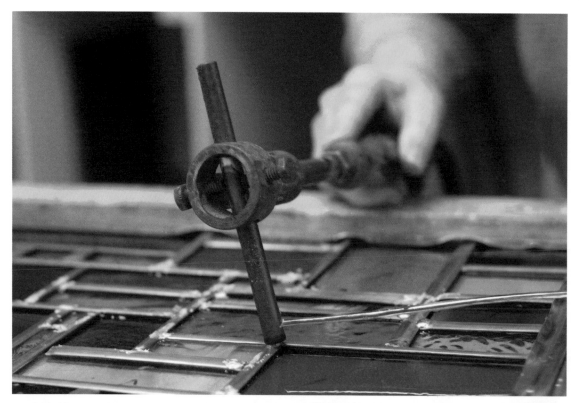

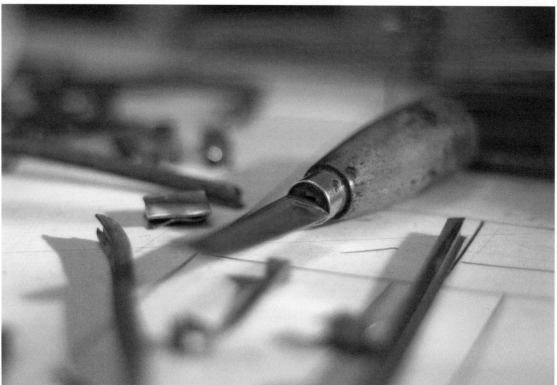

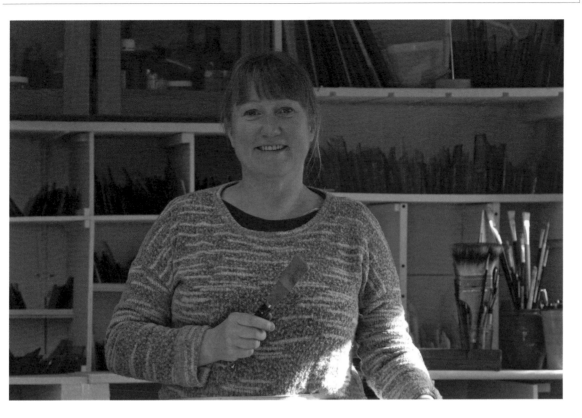

INGER HAMMER, UNITED KINGDOM

AMANDA WINFIELD

Amanda Winfield first acquired her passion for working with stained glass whilst studying at Chelsea School of Art and Design in the early 1980s. Winfield went on to work at renowned stain glass designers Goddard and Gibbs, a firm originally established in 1868, for ten years. By the time she left the firm, Winfield was working as Goddard and Gibbs' studio manager.

Pining for the country, Winfield moved to the beautiful Surrey Hills, where she established her own practice at Abinger Stained Glass in 2001. With the ever changing light of the Surrey sky coming through her workshop's windows Winfield runs courses on a number of different glass working disciplines, as well as continuing her own bespoke work for domestic and commercial clients across the United Kingdom and Europe.

While Winfield is talented enough to have her initials featured in a large heraldic window in London's famous Westminster Abbey, it is her life's work to promote the diversification of stained glass and spread the word that this beautiful medium is not just for churches.

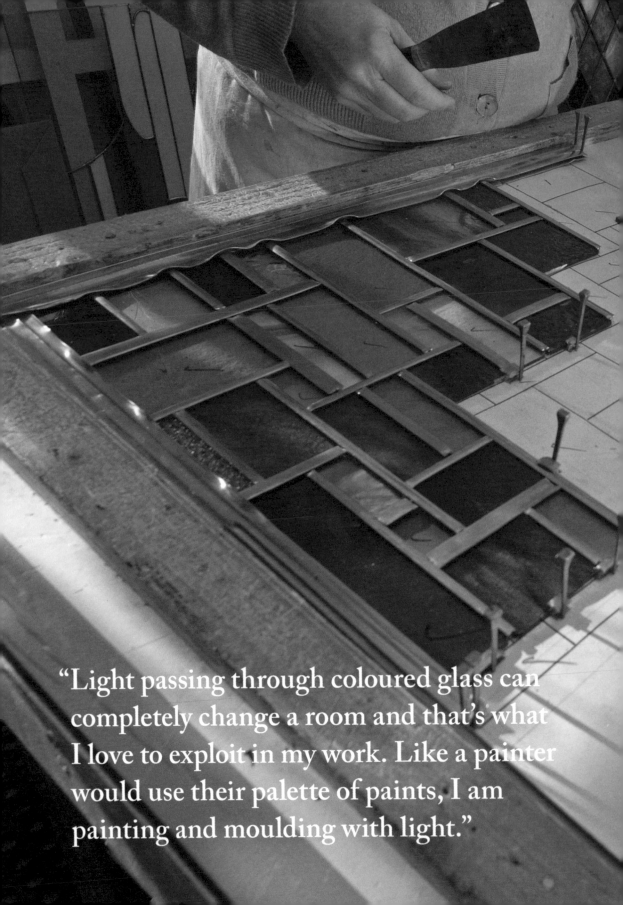

"Light passing through coloured glass can completely change a room and that's what I love to exploit in my work. Like a painter would use their palette of paints, I am painting and moulding with light."

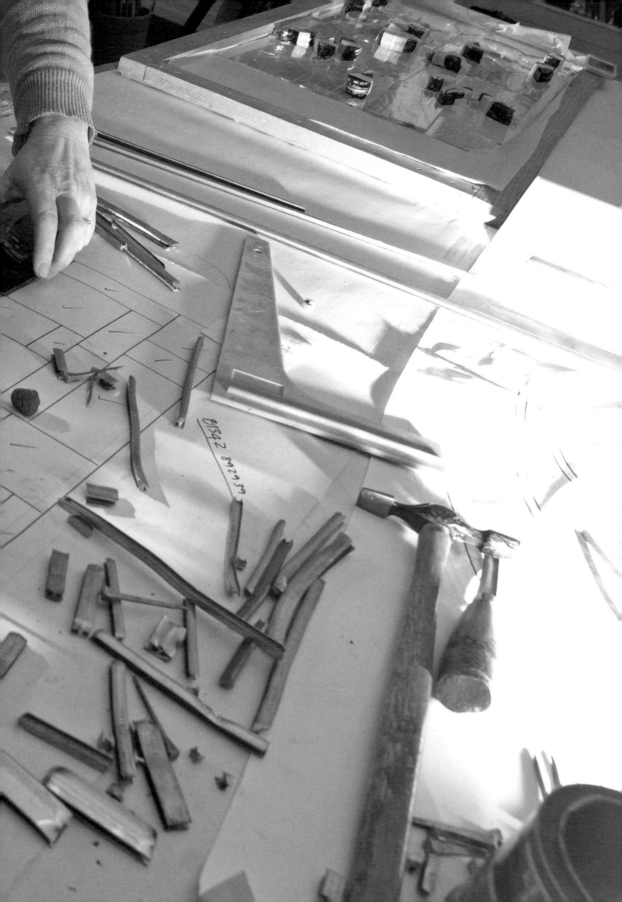

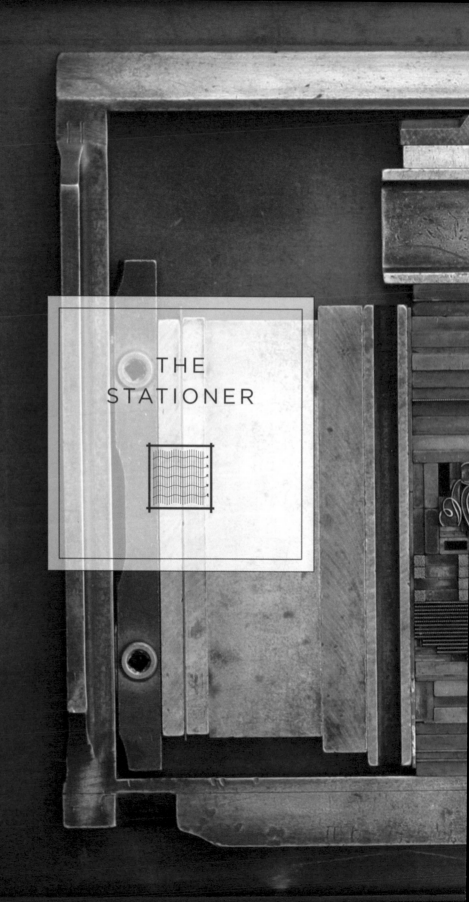

THE
STATIONER

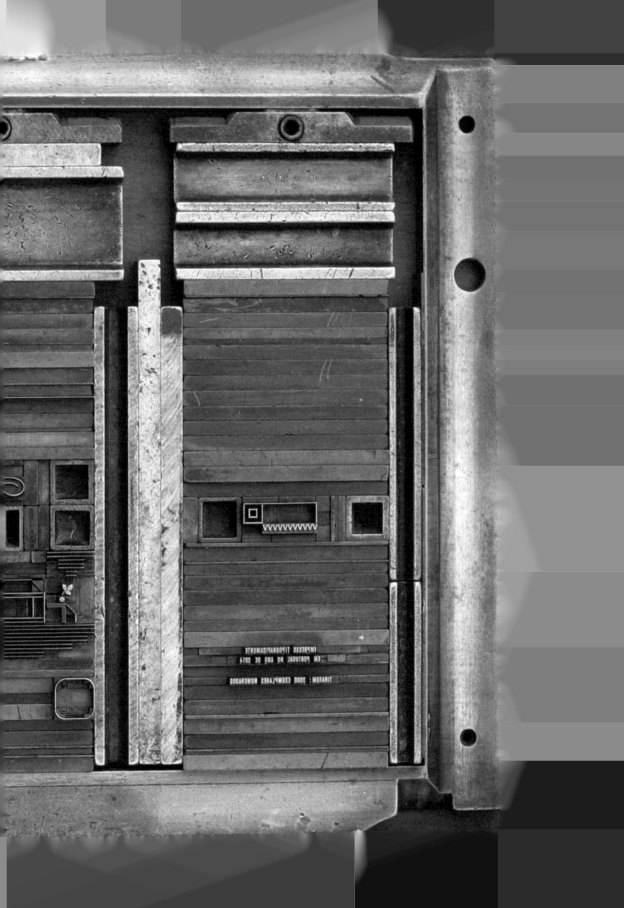

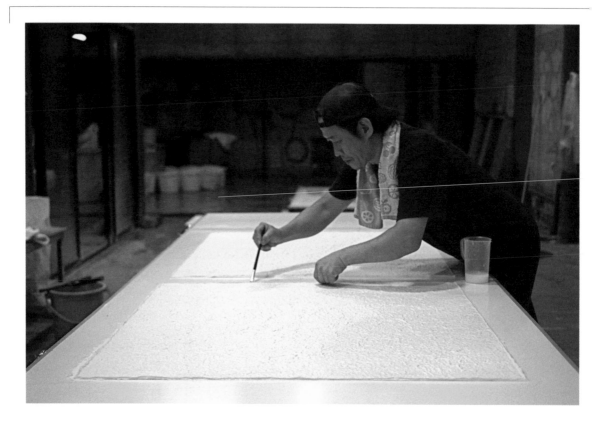

AWAGAMI

Awagami—literally "Paper from Tokushima" (*Awa*, an old name for Tokushima, the area of Japan in which the papermill is located, and *gami*, "paper")—is a family-run business that has operated from the same area for the last 300 years, in a district of Japan in which *Amenohiwashinomikoto* ("the art of paper making") has been practised for over 1,300 years.

Though they produce a number of machine-made papers to meet international demand, the treasure of Awagami's output is their traditional handmade *washi* paper, usually reserved for artists, conservators and specialist printers. This rich, textured paper is produced using materials such as mulberry, bamboo, hemp and the Japanese fibres *gampi* and *mitsumata*, and even, for their superior papers, fibres grown and harvested in the local area.

The equipment and processes Awagami use to create *washi* has barely changed in the centuxries they have operated—though the results vary depending on the individual paper makers working on each batch. To this day the paper is produced using the same method: beaten fibre is added to water and *neri*—a viscous substance gathered from plant roots—and is in constant motion until evenly distributed over a screen surface, from which the paper sheet is taken. This drains overnight and is pressed to remove excess moisture the next day, before being left to dry naturally. At Awagami, finished papers may also be dyed, textured or treated with various solutions to prevent inks used on them from bleeding.

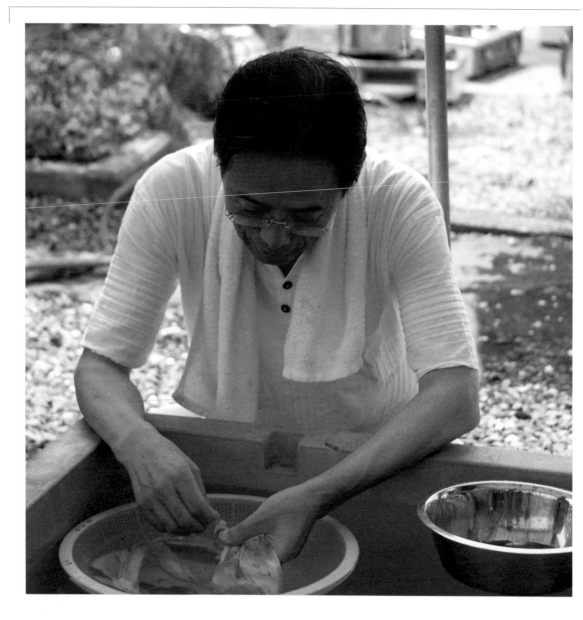

"Only through the skill of past paper making masters did our mill gain recognition."

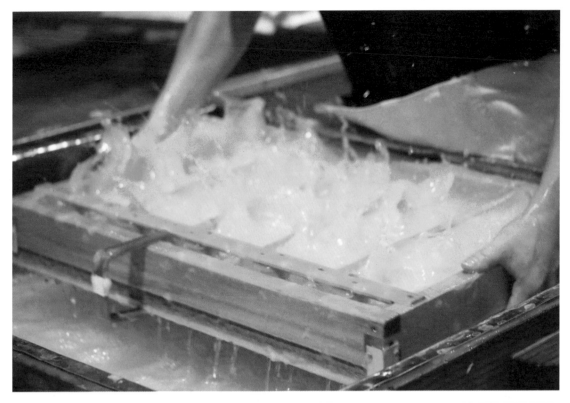

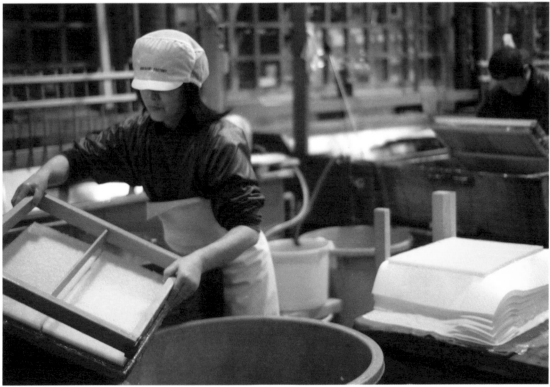

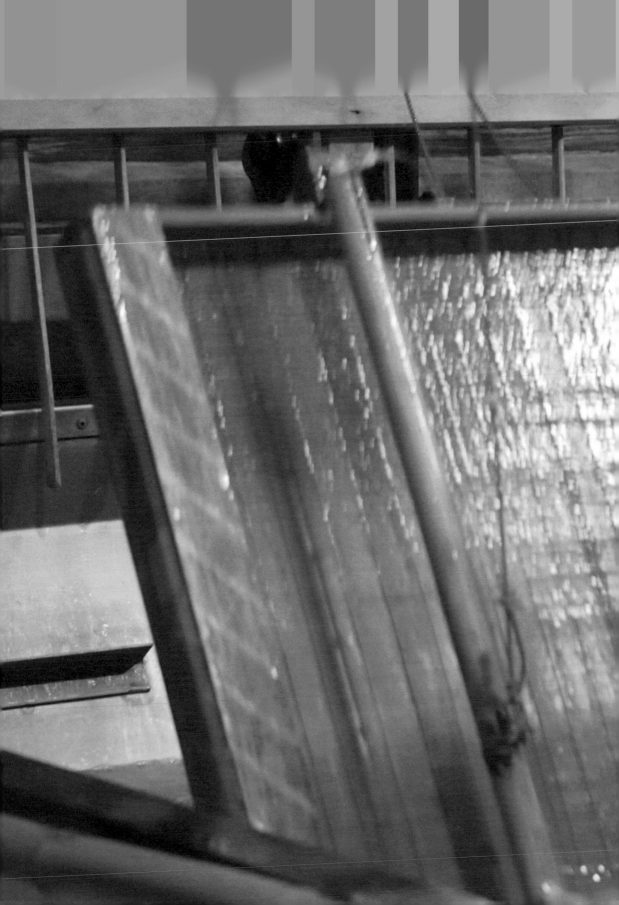

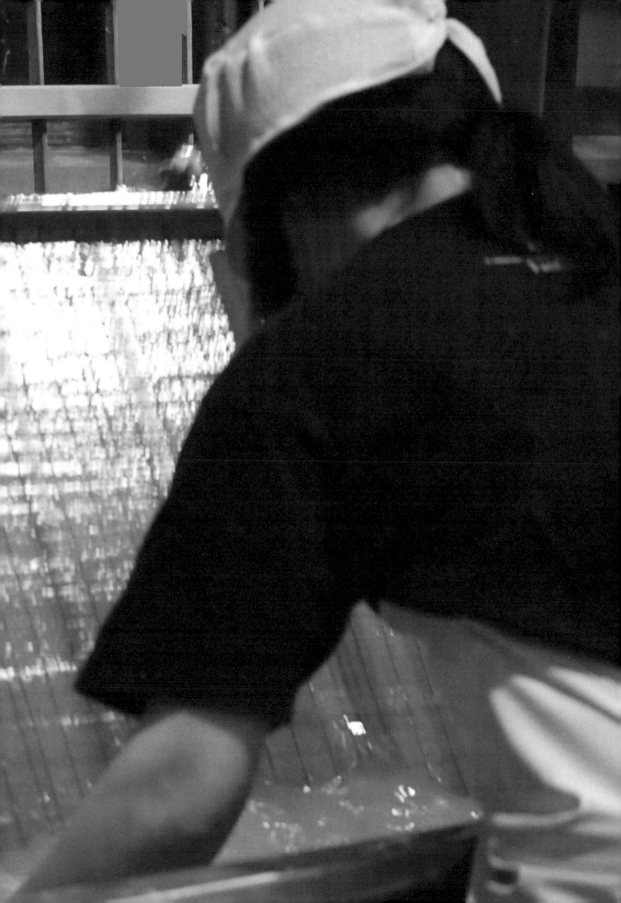

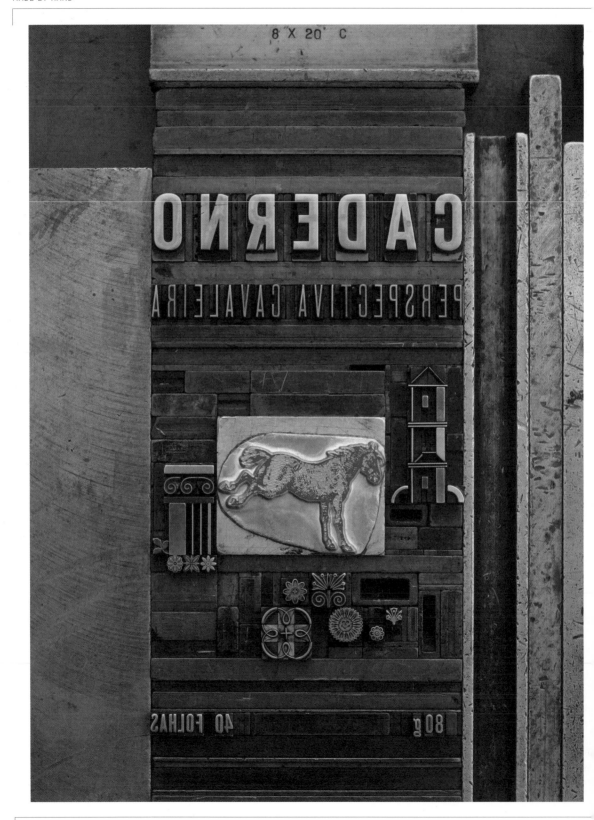

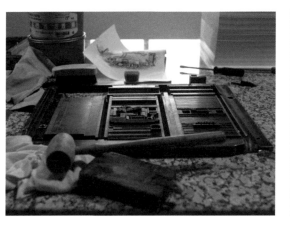
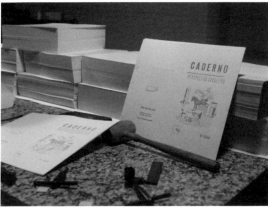

"We are naturally influenced by all the things we have been in contact with since childhood, especially gastronomy, geography, nature and all kinds of old and awkward things."

SERROTE

Undismayed by the decline in traditional letterpress printing—such arduous processes are steadily being replaced with faster, more accurate digital technologies —Lisbon pair, painter and graphic designer Nuno Neves and Susana Vilela, sought out a letterpress and various lead and wood ornaments of their own. Their experiments in the technique, inspired initially by what they call "anonymous design"—old business cards, food packaging, store signs, etc.—have resulted in beautifully individual, handmade notebooks that visually play with Portuguese cultural ephemera, amongst other things.

In Serrote's typical production process, the cover of each notebook goes through the longest procedure of initial concept design, practicality testing, ornament setting in the letterpress and printing—in two parts for two colours—finally being folded, gathered, bound with wire stitching, and trimmed with the other notebook pages.

As well as being somewhat laborious, Neves and Vilela admit that working in letterpress is also rather limiting: they are only able to work with the tools they have to hand. But they charmingly insist that working within such boundaries encourages them to get creative, adapt concepts and materials to meet their needs, and sometimes drop projects, but just as often stumble upon spontaneous ideas as a result of the restrictions.

So why work with a difficult, imperfect process? Neves and Vilela argue that there is a unique quality that comes from handmade letterpress items that they love; the idiosyncratic dints and impressions that old letters have acquired, the difference in print quality due to the pressure of the print or the thickness of the ink, the inevitable little mistakes that happen along the way, all add to the individuality of the piece. And Serrote's notebooks really are individual, each is an individually numbered item in a strictly limited run.

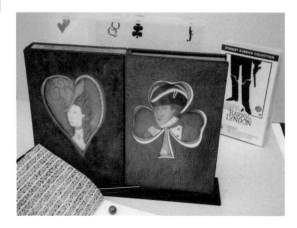
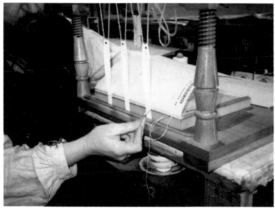

"I immersed myself in my craft, working 40 hours and another 20 overtime, plus the six hours a week in the art evening classes— I loved it."

OAMARU, NEW ZEALAND

MICHAEL O'BRIEN

After Michael O'Brien completed an apprentice in bookbinding and finishing in the early 1980s he moved from Auckland, New Zealand, to London. Choosing between various job offers from renowned London book binders, O'Brien worked for some time at a bindery established on site in the 1780s—whcih he describes as being a "true Victorian sweatshop" complete with Dickensian characters. It was while in London that he began studying in evening courses under the greats of the book binding world, David Sellars and Sally Lou Smith at Bolt Court in Fleet Street.

After two years and having jointly been award the Designer Binder's Award in 1988, O'Brien returned to New Zealand, where he ran a bindery until 1994 when he and his family moved out of the city to a small, South Island Town, Oamaru, where his business has now been established 20 years.

O'Brien is a true master of not only book binding, but also restoration and repair. He uses materials from all over the world in order to achieve the highest quality bindings and period effects. Three of his main bindings, the Dark Age, Cambridge and Gothic bindings, are all sewn the way book bindings were sewn before the 1780s, when an industrial mentality started demanding quicker, less expensive methods. Consequently his binding are stronger and more durable than most handmade books, let alone machine bindings.

O'Brien even has a small stock of antique materials from which he appropriates in certain restoration projects. Other materials used in his exquisite range of books and bindings include gold leaf for edge gilding and leathers from animals as disparate as Nigerian goats, English calfs, possums and even kangaroos. Other cover materials that might appeal include oak and 40,000 year old Kauri preserved in swamp lands.

BOMO ART

Intricate, original hand-drawn illustrations of Budapest landmarks in nineteenth-century splendour, musical scores and traditional style botanical imagery, amongst other things, adorn the hand crafted stationery of Bomo Art.

Bomo Art is the venture of Karoly Boldizsar, who as a child surrounded by paper—his father worked on the fringes of the press industry—soaked up all of its smells and sensations, surrounding himself with labels and stickers of all sorts. With such a love for paper, Boldizsar was never satisfied with the notebooks in which he would write out song lyrics, and set up Bomo Art— which has now had its own tiny stationers in downtown Budapest for 13 years—to make fine notebooks in which writing anything feels good.

It isn't just Bomo Art's hand-drawn designs that make their products special though; Bomo's stationery is entirely made with time-honoured techniques and equipment. They use traditional book stamps, cutting machines and shears, their books are stitched by hand and all of their printing is processed by Hungarian presses. And where necessary, traditional enamellers and carpenters are even drafted in to complete many of Bomo Art's products with an authentic craftsman's touch.

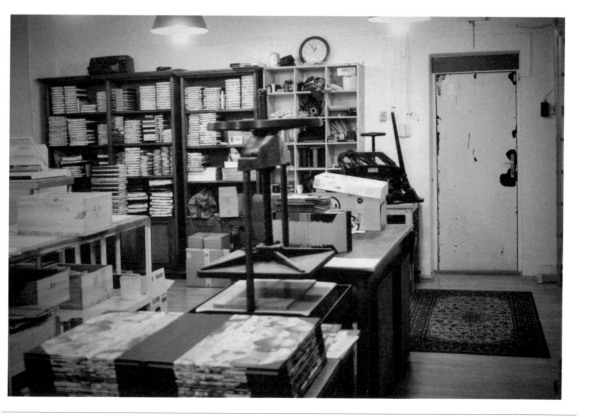

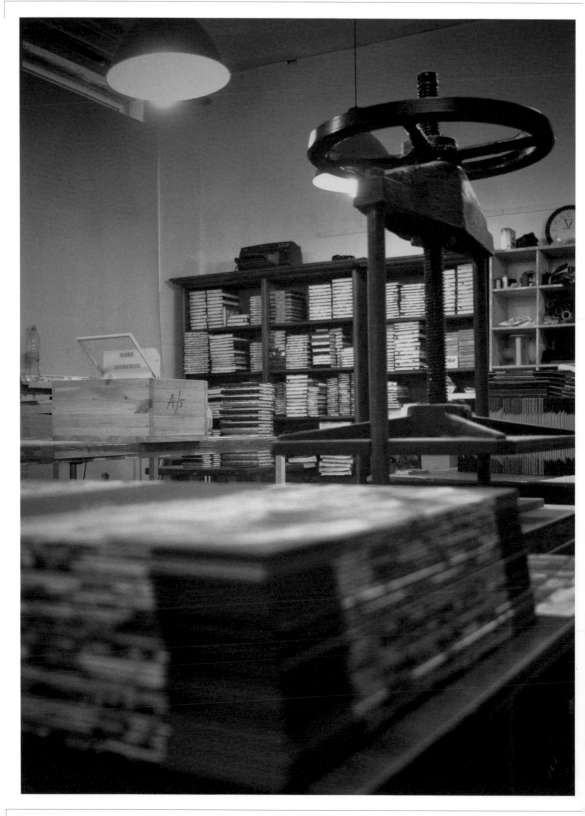

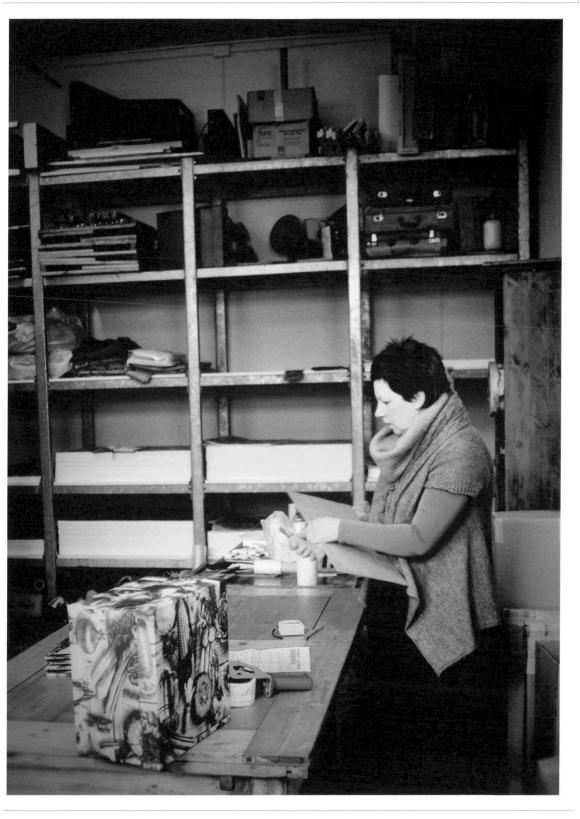

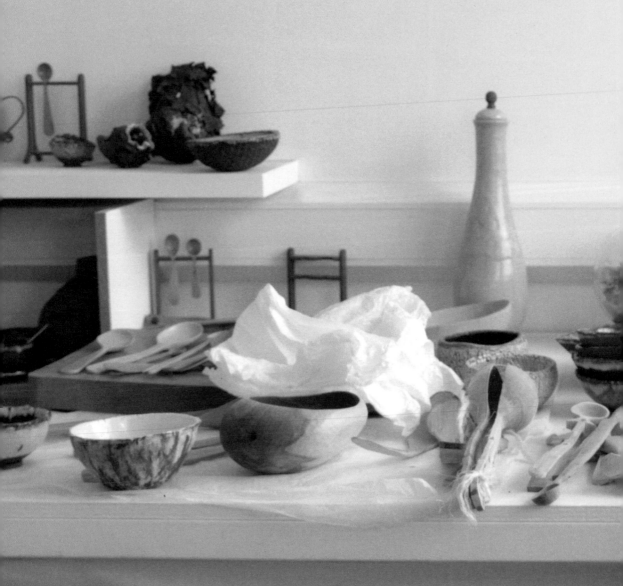

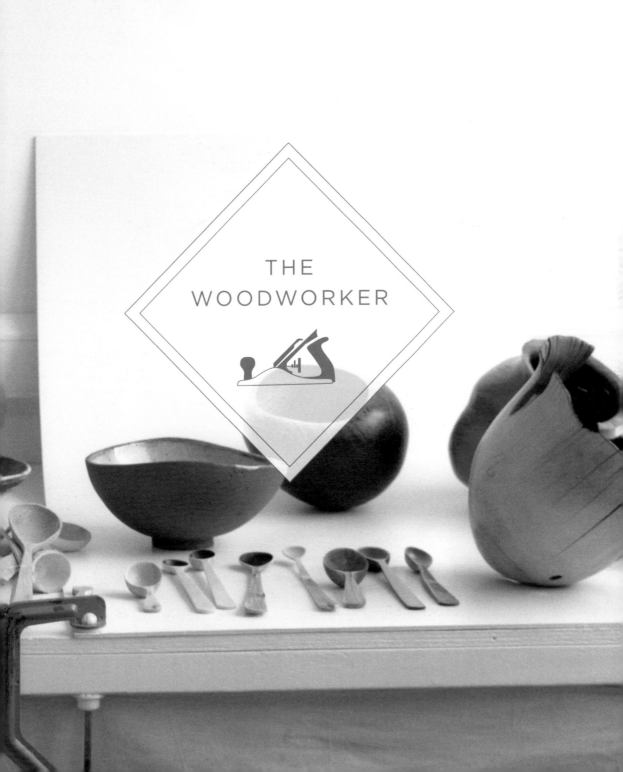

THE
WOODWORKER

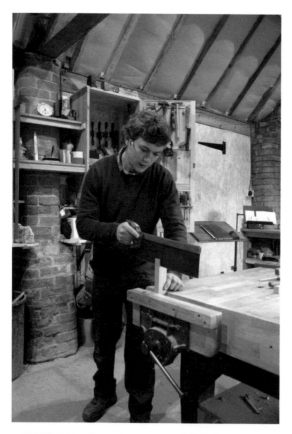

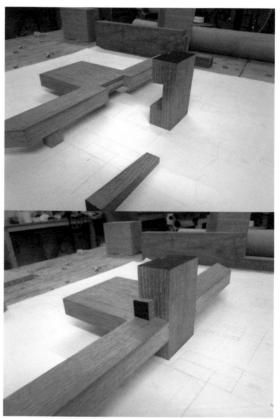

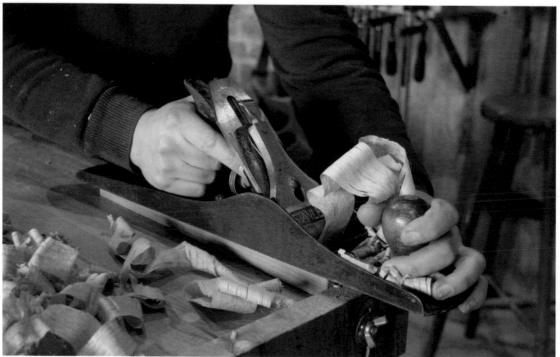

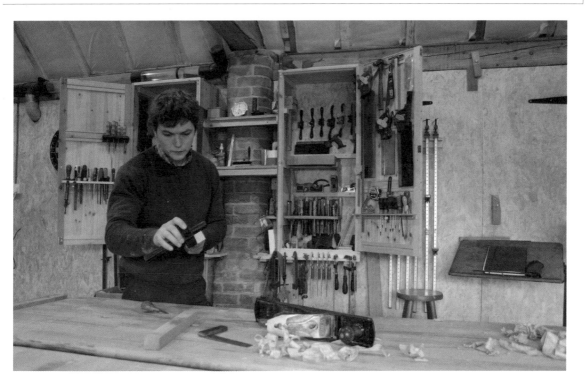

WARWICKSHIRE, UNITED KINGDOM

JOHN EADON

John Eadon has been working with wood since he was a child. Raised on a Warwickshire farm, whittling was a pastime that developed into a natural affinity for wood, and a talent for working with the material from adolescence. Having studied Fine Art at Norwich University of the Arts, Eadon became part of studio collective and gallery start up Stew, where he constructed and maintained a well-equipped workshop, and began making furniture seriously, alongside his practice as a painter. At the same time he was working with a talented boat builder, and assisted on other ambitious projects such as the restoration of Norfolk's Sharington Church's timber frame roof, on behalf of English Heritage.

Now based in a brick outbuilding adjoining the family farm house back in Warwickshire, Eadon makes handmade and bespoke furniture for individual commissions, despite his distaste for the word—"Bespoke is a bit of an over used word really, which it does not necessarily denote high quality, care or even handmade." Every piece of his work is different and is not only loyal to the client's wishes and criteria, but also to the whim's of the material itself. Wood, he maintains, continues a sort of life long after it is felled, as it never ceases moving and reshaping itself as it absorbs and expels moisture in the air.

One of Eadon's particularly challenging commissions was the design and construction of an English oak wardrobe to occupy a deep alcove in the bedroom of a client's very old house. To make things interesting the house had uneven, undulating walls and sloping floors, as well as having been built directly onto the clay, with no foundations. This meant that he needed to produce a wardrobe that could move with the seasonal movements of the building without the joints coming loose or breaking, as glued, nailed or screwed joints would. Eadon answer was to design a wedged joint (pictured) that would flex, and loosen under stress, and that could be tightened with a quick whack of the mallet. Only making things entirely by hand, on a project-by-project basis, allows for this sort of attention to detail and custom perfection.

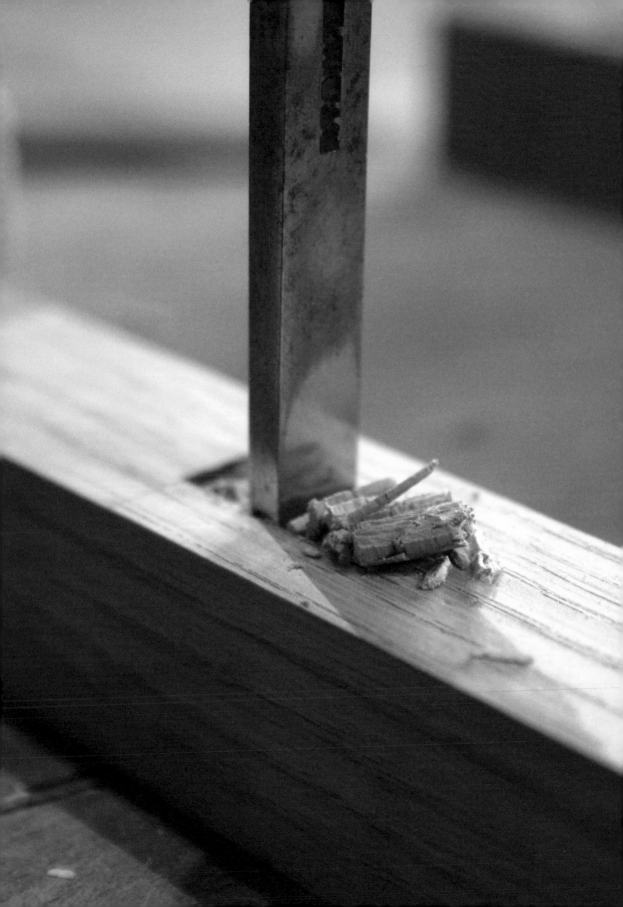

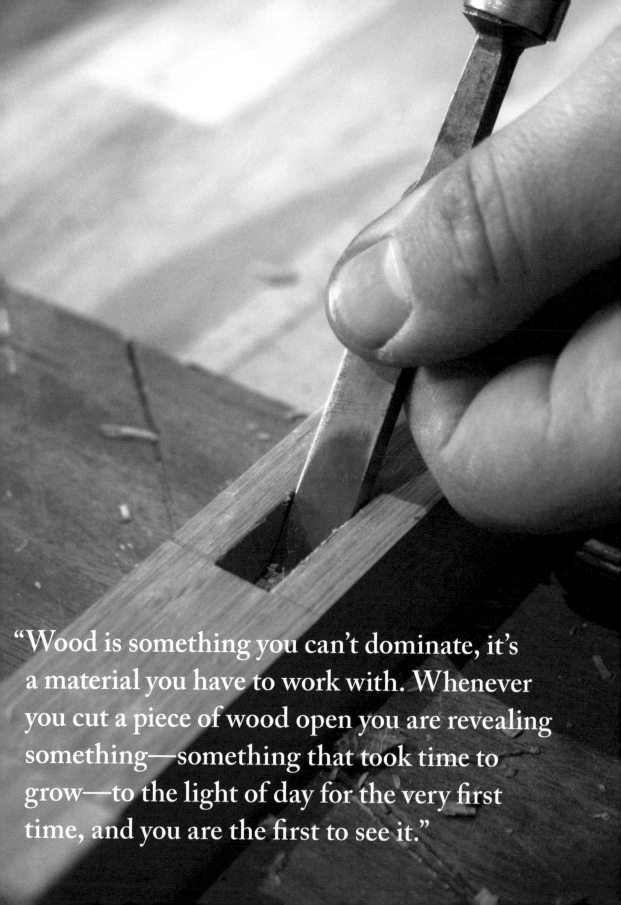

"Wood is something you can't dominate, it's a material you have to work with. Whenever you cut a piece of wood open you are revealing something—something that took time to grow—to the light of day for the very first time, and you are the first to see it."

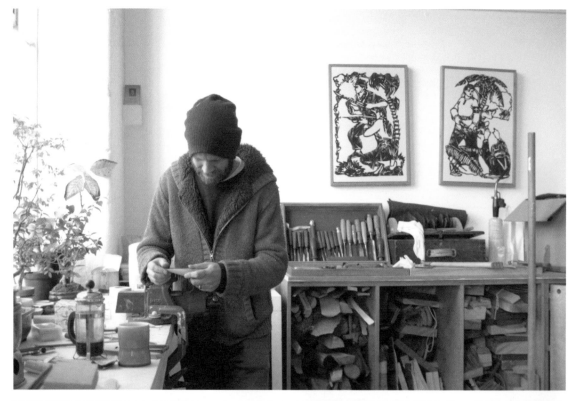

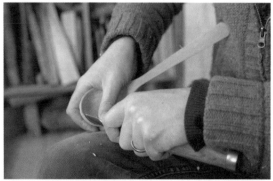

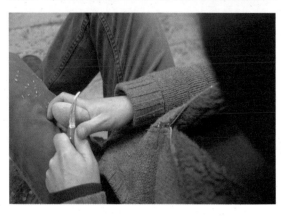

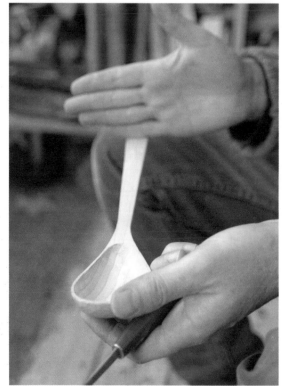

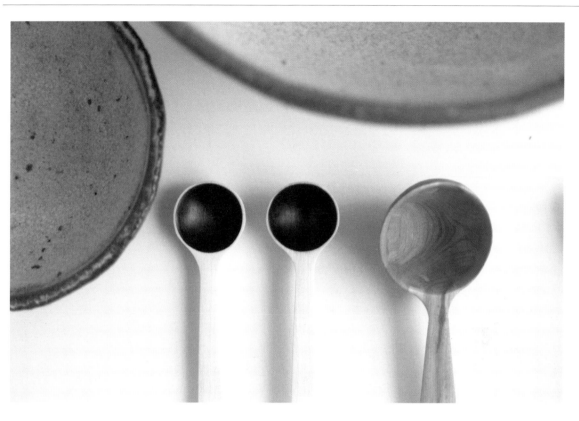

●NDON, UNITED KINGDOM

NIC WEBB

Nic Webb is a true master of materials. Having studied painting at Brighton University, he wanted to work more explicitly with his hands. He started working with wood and fell in love with the breadth of possibility that the material provided. His investigation into wood's properties is truly expansive. He has studied, in finite detail, its aging process, its reaction to the elemental forces of fire and ice, its functionality, and the ways in which it has been used by humankind with an almost anthropological obsession.

The bread and butter of his practice are his spoons. He carves spoons from green (freshly cut and still moist) wood, allowing him a freedom given the suppleness of this wood—as opposed to dried wood. Green wood also introduces to the process the excitement of working with a material that is still living, moving, expanding and contracting. Webb's spoons are a way of fulfilling his interest in the functionality of wood, and examining the pure and concise relationship between maker and material. There is nothing purer than making a 'tool' like a spoon, an object of complete functionality. Yet Webb also subverts this aspect of his work by making spoons that are breathtakingly beautiful and arguably ornamental.

Aside from his spoons, he is keen to talk studio visitors through any number of his bizarre and fascinating experiments with wood. Huge wooden vessels, resembling giant petrified flowers, are made by blowing air into a cavity in a huge log which has red hot embers in it. Once Webb is satisfied by the warped and undulating chasm burnt within, he lets the embers die, and then begins removing wood from the outside of the log until its walls are paper-thin. Other experiments include firing ceramics in crude, home made kilns, wherein he mixes ashes from the kiln's embers into glazes used on the finished ceramics. Poignantly, Webb tries, where he can, to remove the wood, with which he powers the kiln, and the clay, with which he makes the ceramics, from the same site.

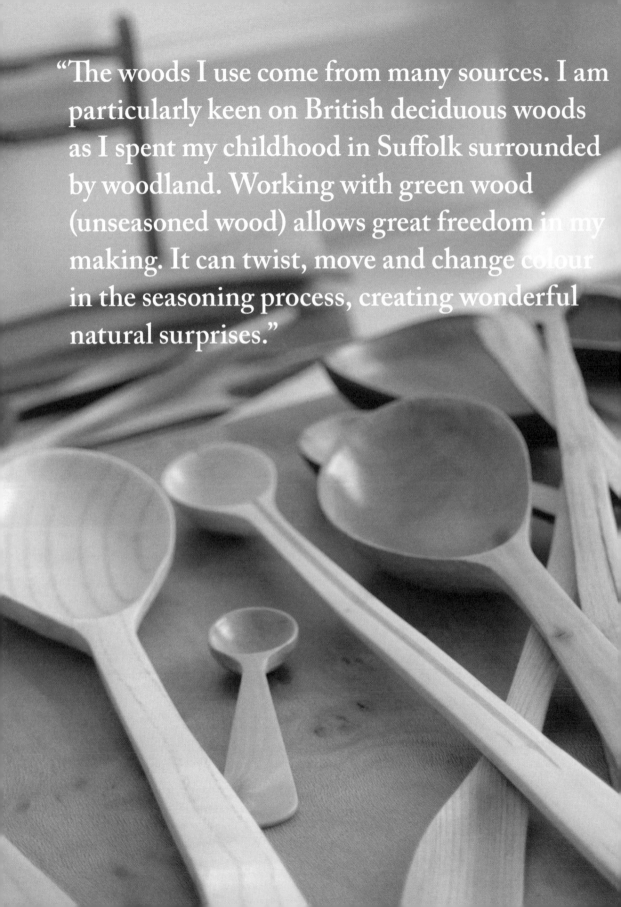

"The woods I use come from many sources. I am particularly keen on British deciduous woods as I spent my childhood in Suffolk surrounded by woodland. Working with green wood (unseasoned wood) allows great freedom in my making. It can twist, move and change colour in the seasoning process, creating wonderful natural surprises."

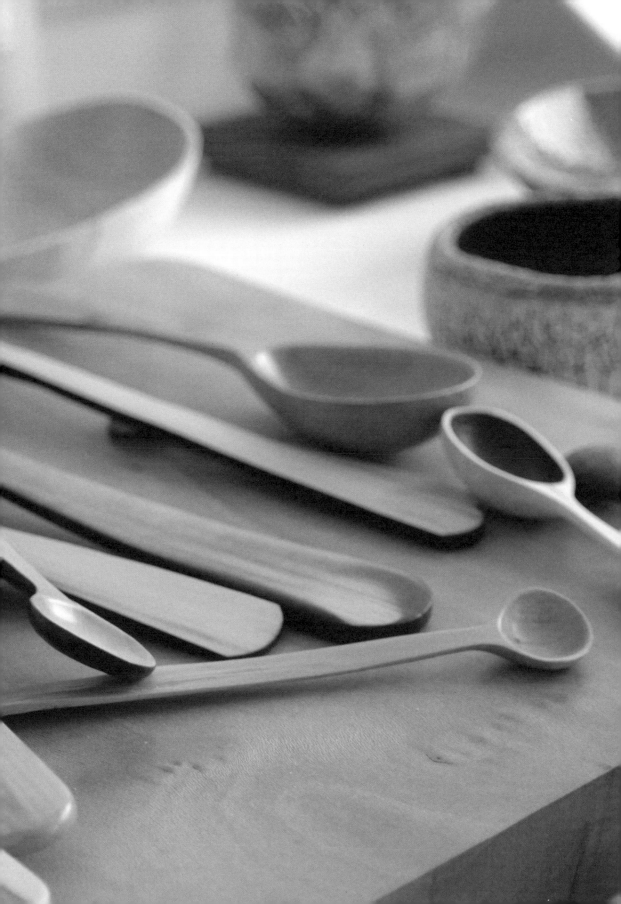

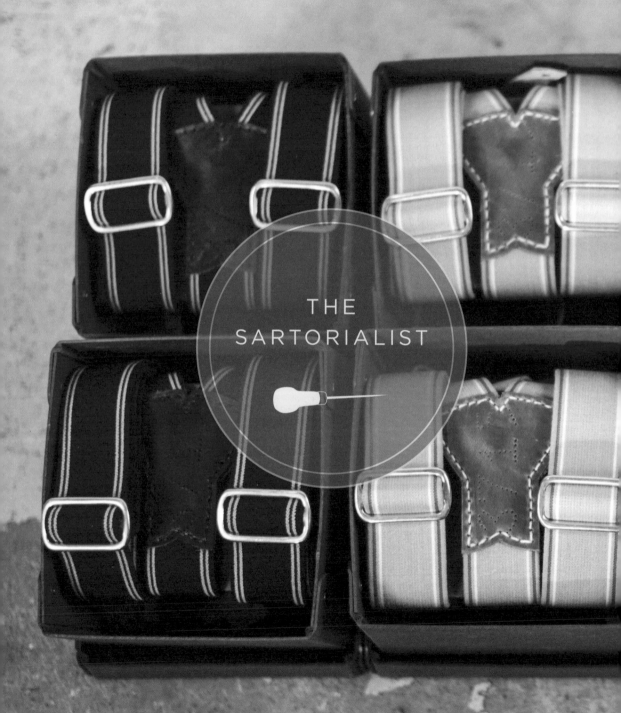

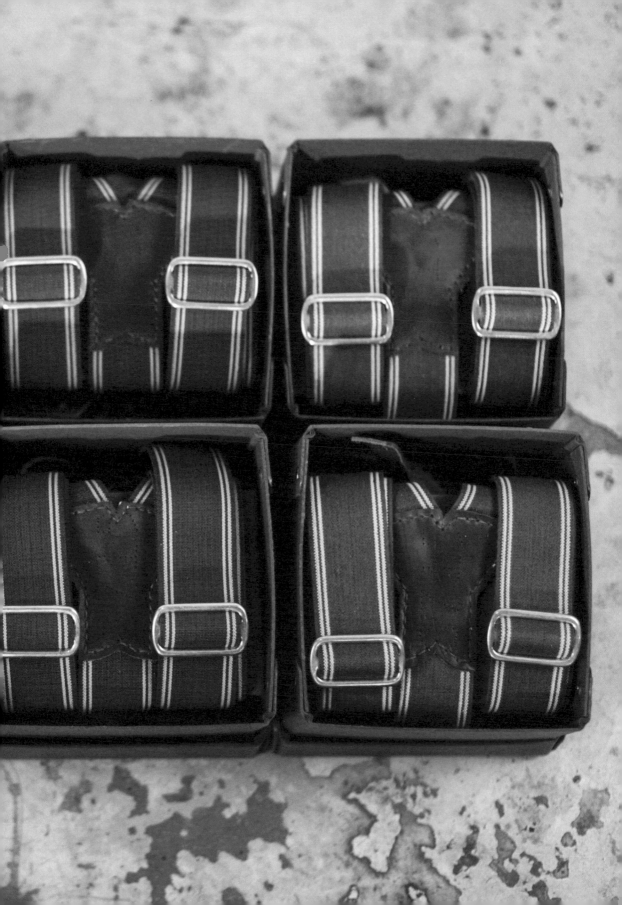

ELLA BING BOW TIES

Ella Bing bow ties was started in 2010 by Lisa and Brent Kraus as a means by which to honour and remember his brother Matthew, who had recently passed. Matthew, it seems, was something of an ambassador for bow ties, wearing them frequently in place of the more popular necktie. After his brother's passing Brent began wearing some of his brother's collection and soon understood his fanaticism about the unique feeling they give you. Now, several years on, Ella Bing produce several ranges of bow ties including reversible models and even those made of wood.

The company, operating out of Tampa Bay, Florida, prides itself on its unique approach to hand making bow ties, with Brent himself making every single tie that goes out. Certain lines contain stock models, but others have one off, unique bow ties allowing wearers that smug feeling of absolute certainty that no one else has the piece they are wearing.

Ella Bing's website is something of a hub for bow tie wearers, offering advice on how to tie them, what to where them with and even hosting a monthly bow tie club! So dedicated to the promotion of bow ties is the company, in fact, that they even run an initiative called "The Necktie Eradication Project", whereby if customers send in old neckties to be converted into bow ties, Ella Bing will sell you your bow tie at a reduced rate.

Most famous for their 'woodys', or wooden bow ties, Ella Bing use rare and unusual hard woods from all over the planet and, unlike a lot of companies that make wooden bow ties, they hand shape each one individually, with no laser cutting used. Every Ella Bing bow tie that is sent out is shipped in a vintage cigar box, very apt given their location in Tampa Bay, the United States' cigar capital.

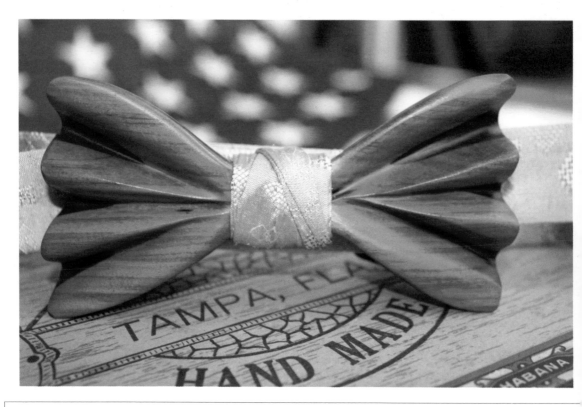

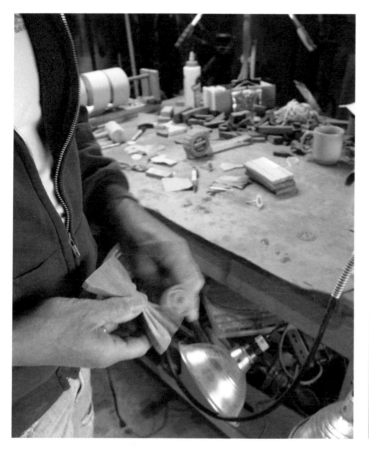
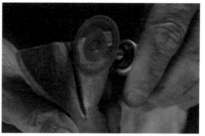
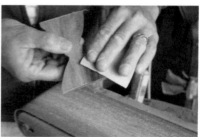
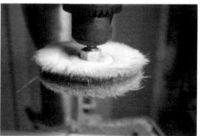

"In the beginning we were looking for different ways to involve my dad. He is a very talented wood worker. So we googled around to see what people were doing with wooden bow ties. There wasn't much. So we ran with it."

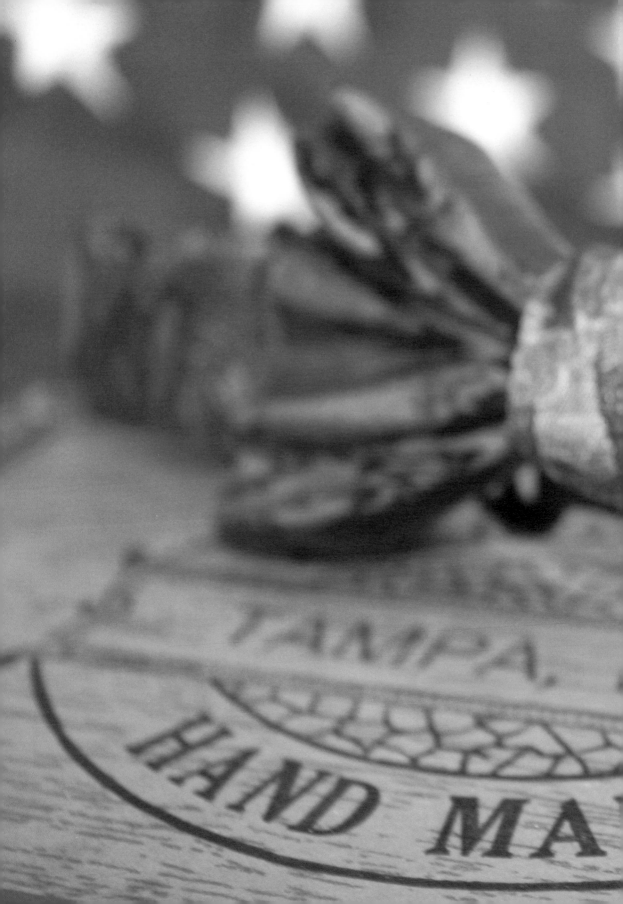

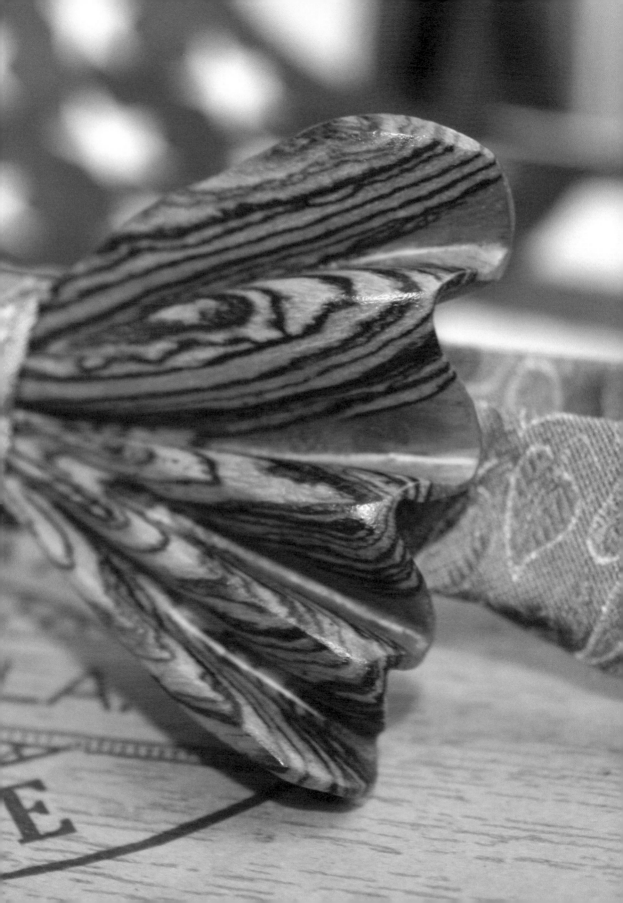

"It's important to aim for the highest quality components possible and use components that support the story for the products, using local manufacturers supports the personal and geographical story I use for my products."

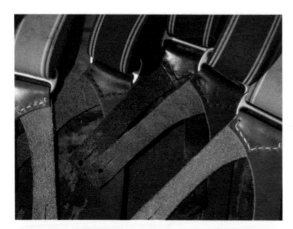

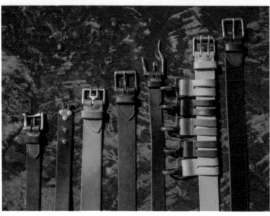

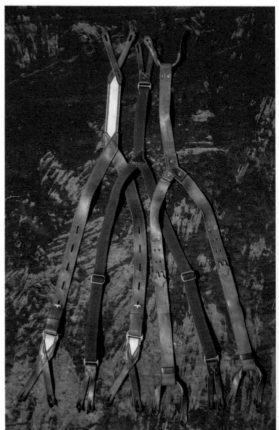

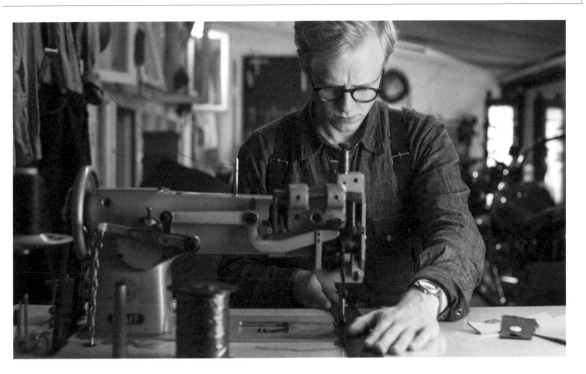

OPENHAGEN, DENMARK

FOR HOLDING UP THE TROUSERS

A belt or pair of suspenders from Morten Kristensen's company, For Holding Up The Trousers, could not be more different to a belt or pair of suspenders bought 'off the rail'. The components and fastenings that he uses are mostly reclaimed hardware, either rifle sling hooks or hardware more typically found in an equestrian harness maker's parts bin. The leather used in making his belts is heavy weight, industrial thickness with unburnished edges. The stitching, patterns and designs that For Holding Up The Trousers' products employ are as progressive as they could be, while still remaining totally dedicated to comfort and functionality.

Kristensen started the company after dropping out of the London College of Fashion and subsequently interned at London design brand Tender Co.. He initially made some belts for a friend who had opened a collective shop in Copenhagen called Mall. When the belts sold through pretty quickly Kristensen made more, and then started working on suspenders too. For Holding Up The Trousers takes inspiration from nineteenth century Americana and industrial work wear, and so all of his designs are rough and durable, a belt of his will last you a lifetime.

Kristensen had done some leatherwork as a child and was raised by creative parents, both ceramicists, who encouraged a pursuit of the applied arts. Toying with scraps of leather from a sack full of off-cuts, the nascent maker was very young when he finished his first belt. The farm on which Kristensen's parents raised him was originally a pig farm, and on the property he found an old branding stamp denoting the number '3715'. All the pigs sent out of this farm would have been branded 3715, and now Kristensen brands each and every of his products with it.

While For Holding Up The Trousers is known for its unique designs and unorthodox approaches to traditional belts and suspenders, the use of high quality and well manufactured materials is equally important to Kristensen's vision. The elastics he uses are woven in England, he uses buckles cast in England and Germany and leather that is tanned in Sweden. While Kristensen is not able to use truly local produce, because of Denmark's relative lack of manufacturing, the products come from companies who have been making their components for many years and using solid raw materials to produce a product of top quality.

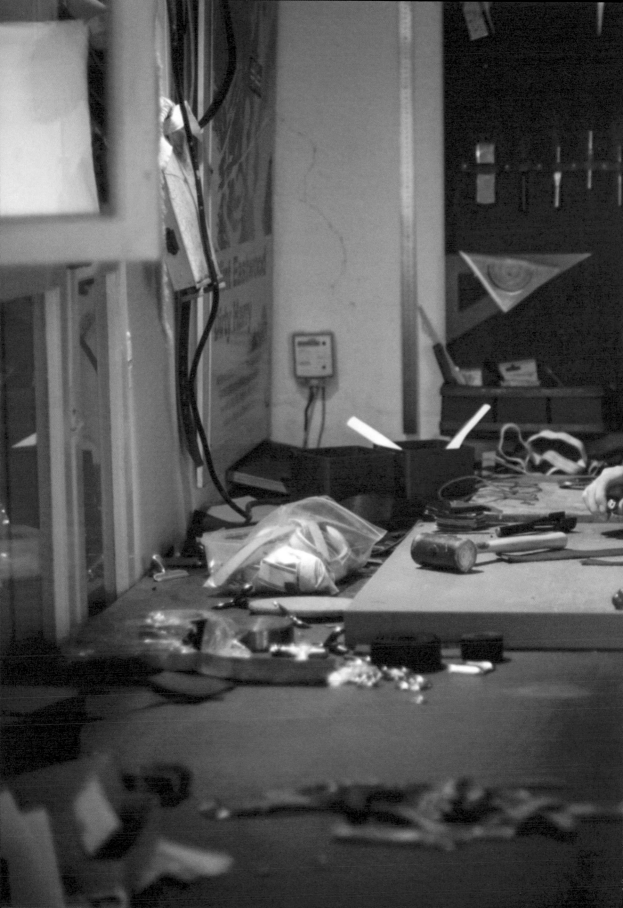

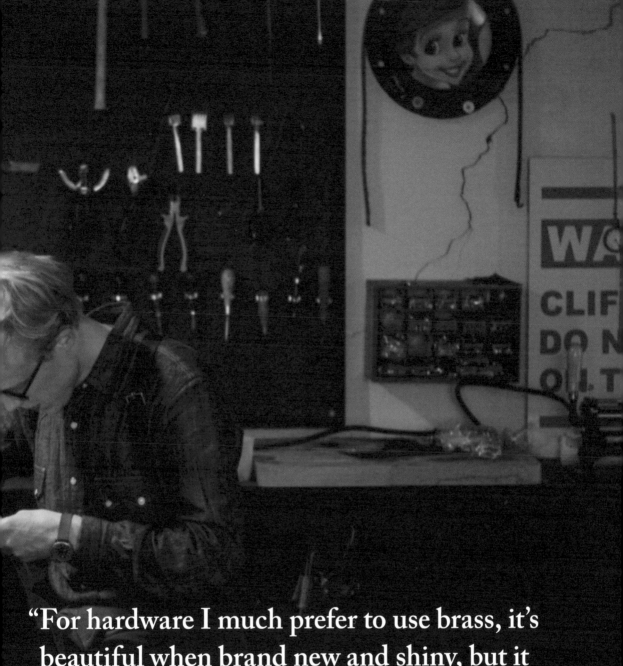

"For hardware I much prefer to use brass, it's beautiful when brand new and shiny, but it will be even better down the line when it's all dull and carries the marks of its use, the same way the leather ages and ends up with

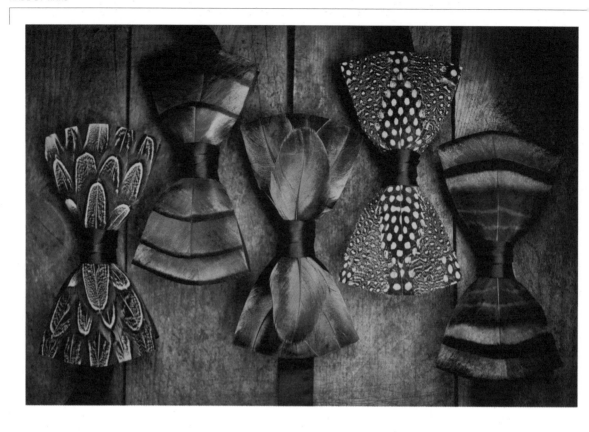

BRACKISH

Charleston-based bow tie producers, Brackish, have created an accessories collection with a distinctive taste of South Carolina's great outdoors. The company was founded by Jeff Plotner and Ben Ross on the success of Ross's first experimental turkey feather bow ties— handmade by himself as innovative and personal gifts for the groomsmen at his wedding.

Today Brackish bow ties are handmade by a small team of local artisans, each with their own skills and perfected methods that translate into one of a kind pieces. The intricate production process—in which the feathers are individually hand selected for each bow tie —requires a high level of quality hand craft and can take between four and five hours to complete.

While using feathers in itself provides a characteristic natural aesthetic, many of the feathers used are actually from birds native to the South Carolina region (though, as the company's production has increased they have started sourcing feathers from across the United States —an aid to small time farms who would usually have to dispose of them).

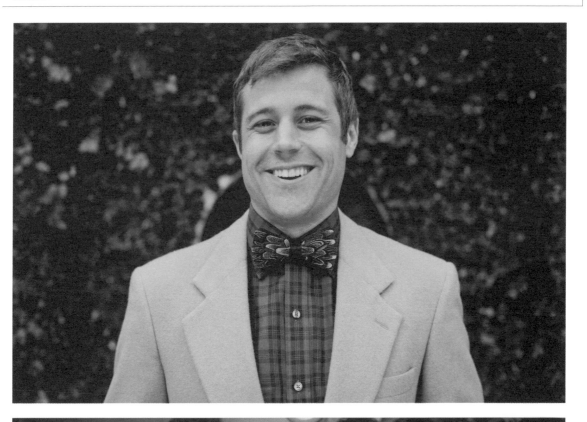

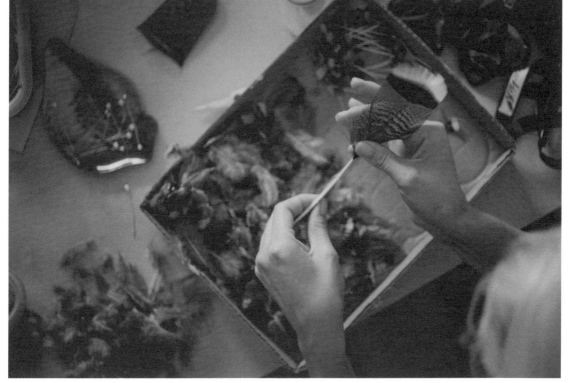

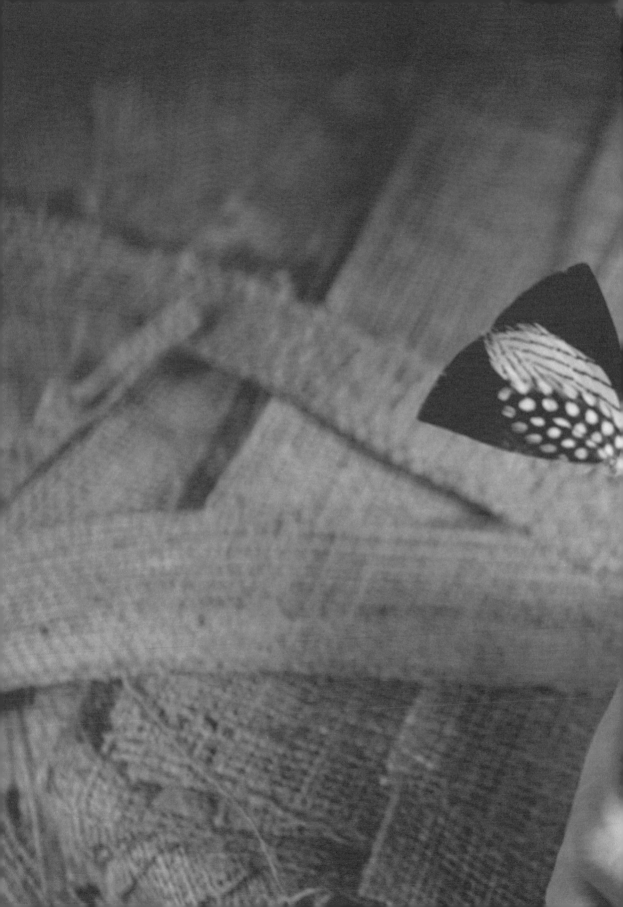

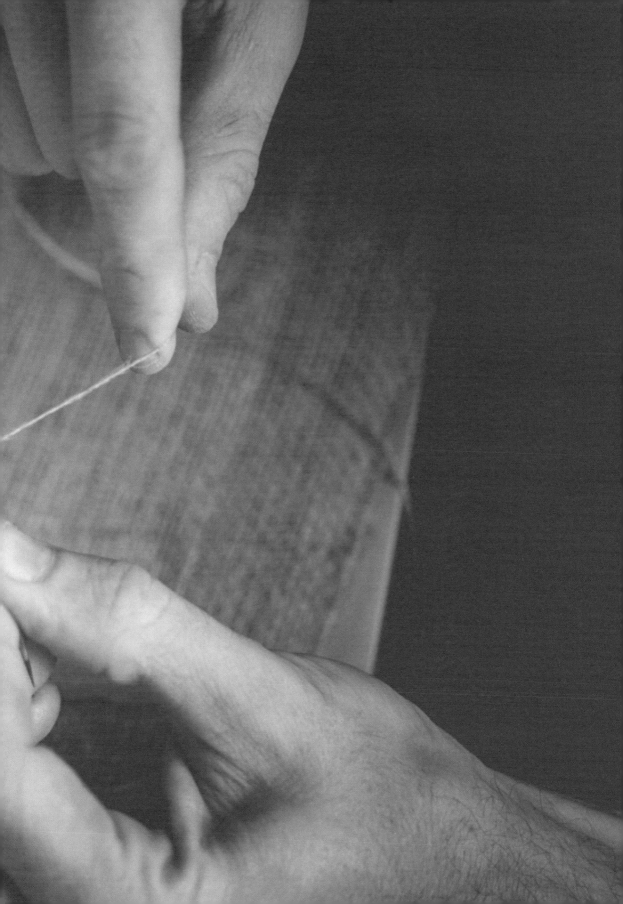

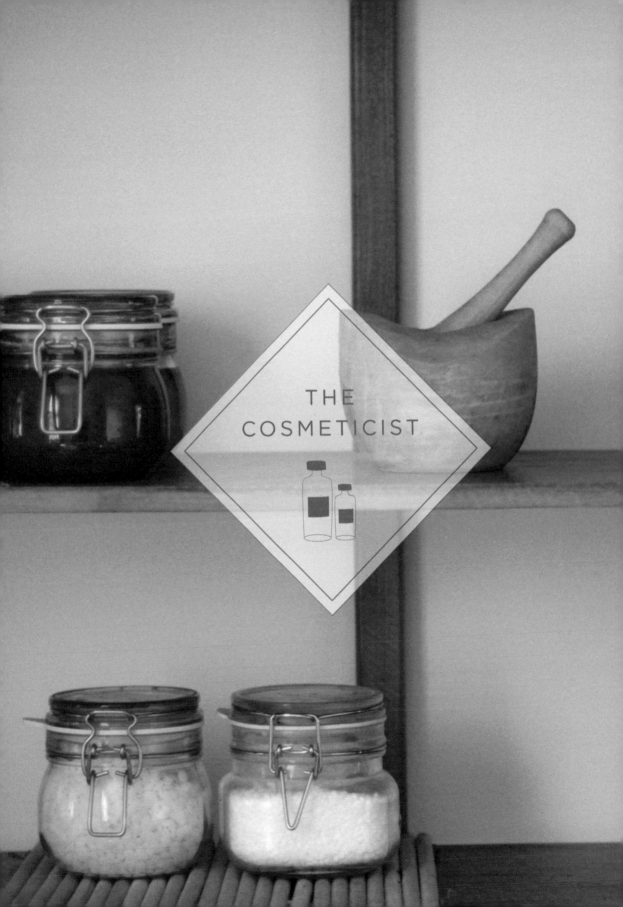

THE
COSMETICIST

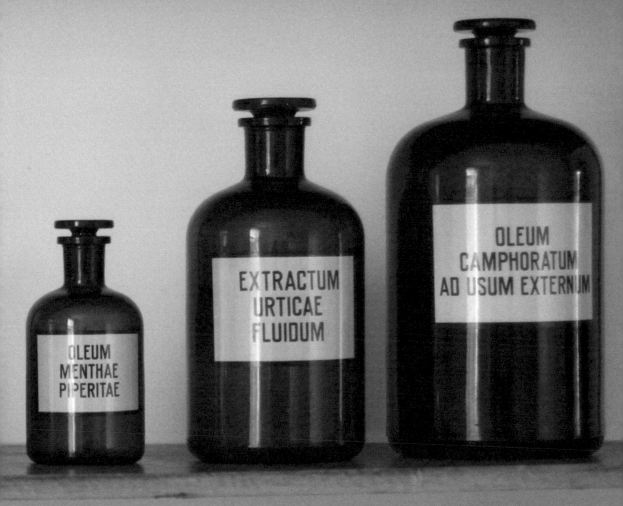

OLEUM
MENTHAE
PIPERITAE

EXTRACTUM
URTICAE
FLUIDUM

OLEUM
CAMPHORATUM
AD USUM EXTERNUM

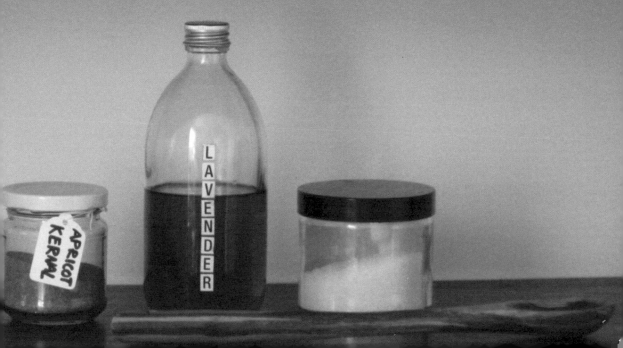

APRICOT
KERNAL

LAVENDER

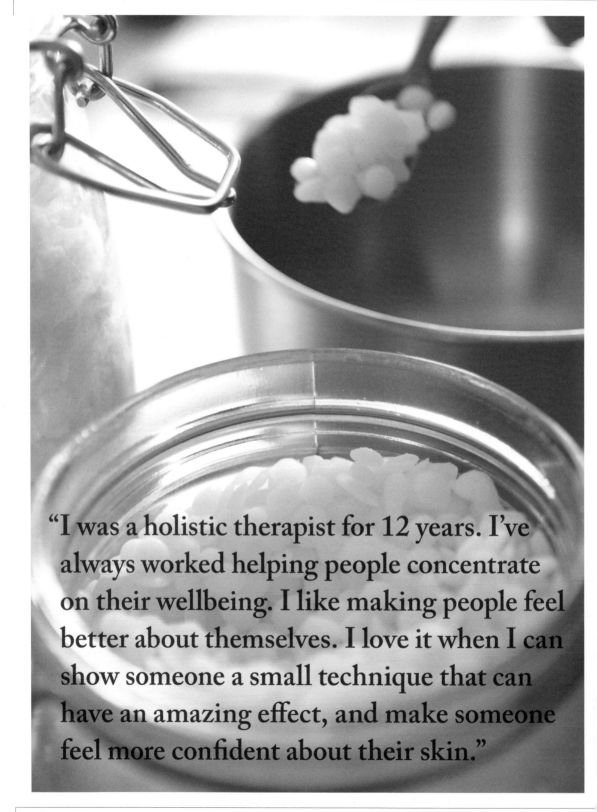

"I was a holistic therapist for 12 years. I've always worked helping people concentrate on their wellbeing. I like making people feel better about themselves. I love it when I can show someone a small technique that can have an amazing effect, and make someone feel more confident about their skin."

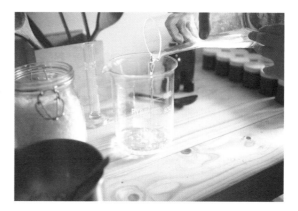

HONEST SKINCARE

Katie Fisher works from a small studio in Birmingham. Surrounded by shelves of natural ingredients, packaging materials and mixing tools, Fisher's calming space is part apothecary, part holistic retreat, for both her and her customers.

Before studying natural skincare Fisher was working as a holistic therapist. Making people feel at ease with themselves but also having an inherent ability to understand wellbeing remains her trade to this day. She uses simple but perfectly balanced selections of natural materials to produce skincare packages in small batches. The products' shorter shelf lives are testament to their purity compared to mass-produced and more widely available products—long shelf lives equating high levels of petrochemicals and preservatives, and a less than natural treatment for the user's skin. Fisher independently sources organic butters, waxes and vitamins and mixes them with essential oils to produce treatments that work with the skin's biology to nourish, protect and restore it.

Fisher has sensitive skin herself, which reacts badly to certain products, and was disappointed to discover her skin did not agree with off-the-shelf products advertised as 'organic' or 'natural'. This was her initial reasoning for looking closely at natural skincare and embarking upon its study. One of the primary lessons learnt was to always closely examine what even the most supposedly organic products contain. This faithfulness to natural, raw ingredients has become an essential part of Honest Skincare's branding, and Fisher favours the use of woods, stone, glass and linen in her packaging—simple on the outside, simple on the inside.

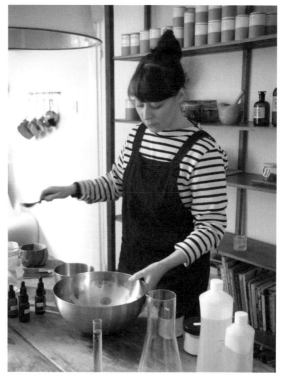

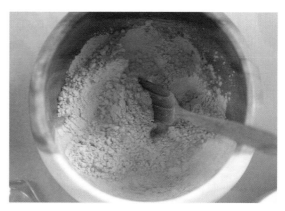

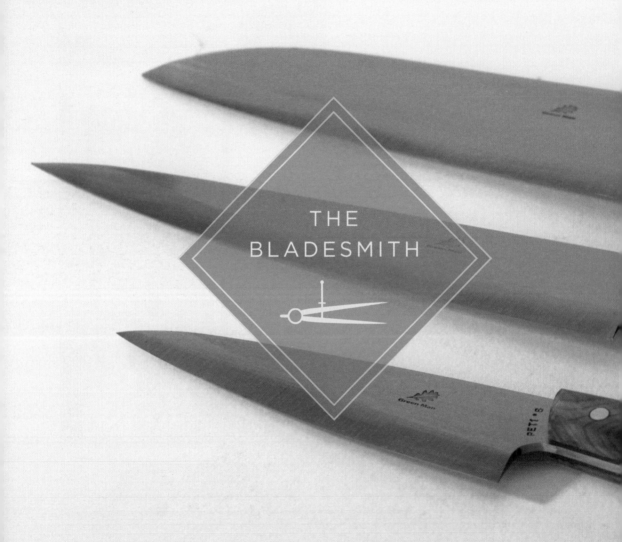

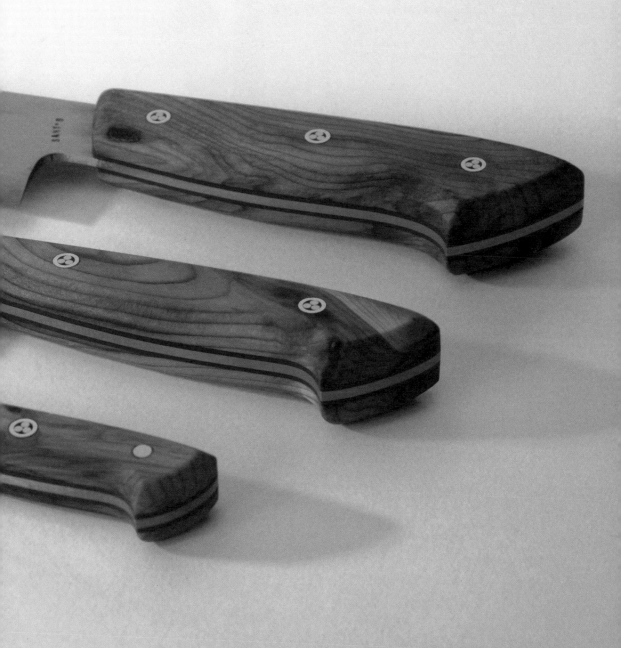

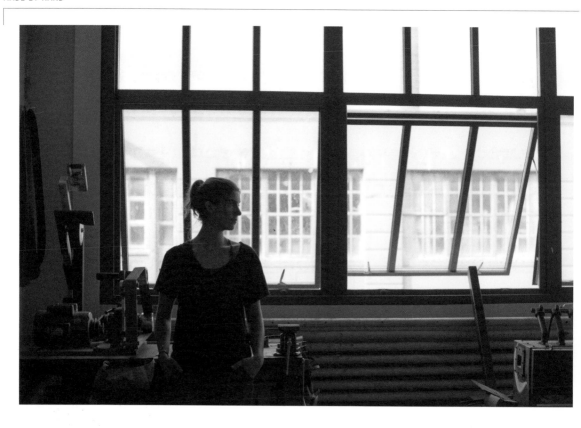

BROOKLYN, UNITED STATES

ORCHARD STEEL

Moriah Cowles of Orchard Steel is originally from Vermont, where her family have been operating an apple orchard since the 1940s. When she established her knife making practice in Brooklyn, it seemed a logical decision to name her work after her home. She would be using wood from her parents' orchard for the knife handles, after all.

Cowles developed a taste for blacksmithing whilst studying art, and was introduced to knife making whilst on a cycling trip through Mexico, taking an apprenticeship with a bladesmith for six weeks. Via a meandering route she found herself in Brooklyn, working for and learning from renowned culinary knife maker Joel Bukiewicz of Cut Brooklyn. Cowles now operates her own business making a refined line of her own culinary knives, a paring knife, petty knife and larger chef's knife. The knives continue some of the most unusual and interesting designs available, fusing the styles of Japanese Gyoto knives with French Sabatier knives.

Cowles heats basic tool steel to around 1600 °C in her forge, before using a hammer and anvil to beat the glowing metal into the rough shape of her knife. She will get the knife's shape as close as possible to the finished article with the hammer, before finishing the blade's profile on a belt sander. Once the holes are drilled for the handle attachment the blade receives a heat treatment and tempering, processes which heat and cool the metal, changing its molecular structure and achieving an optimum hardness. Then the handles can be added and the blade finally sharpened.

"Just like the tomatoes you buy from the farmer's market, knowing where your knife comes from not only gives you a personal connection to the knife, the maker and his or her story, but it also allows you to hold the maker accountable for their product."

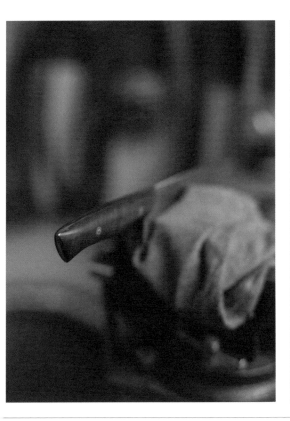
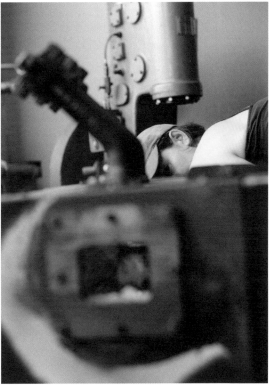

"Having something that lasts a long time, and being able to place a face to the hands that made it, is becoming more and more valuable. We want to have less stuff, and the stuff we choose to surround ourselves with to hold more meaning."

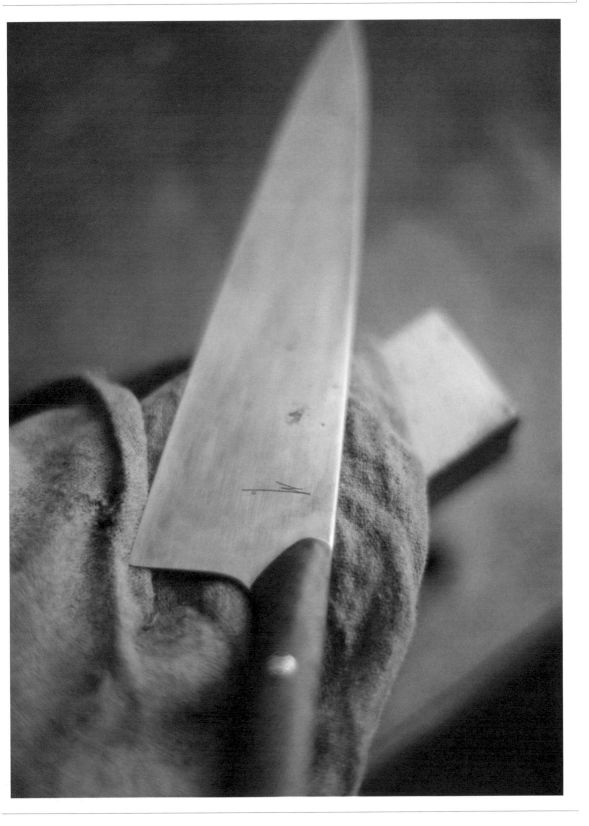

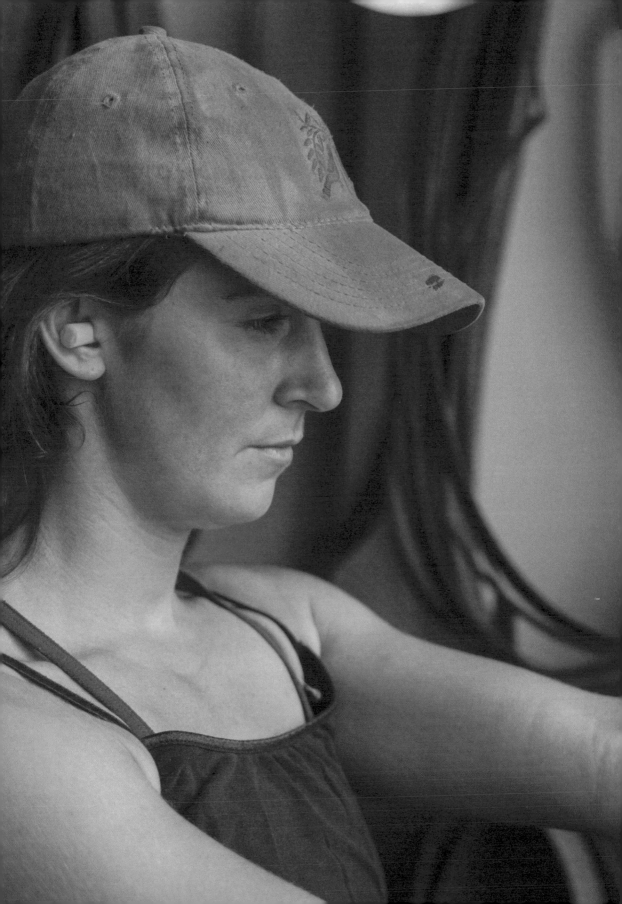

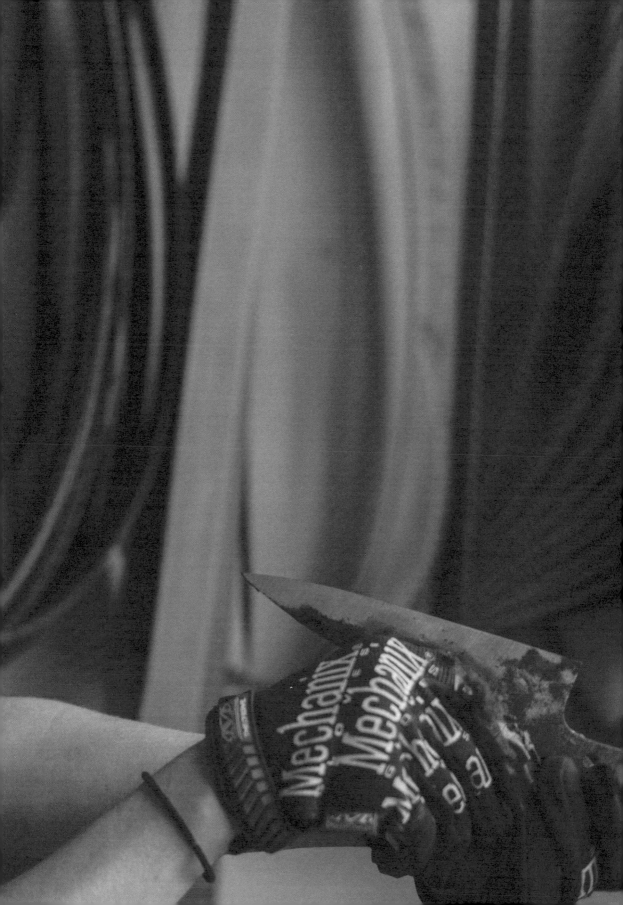

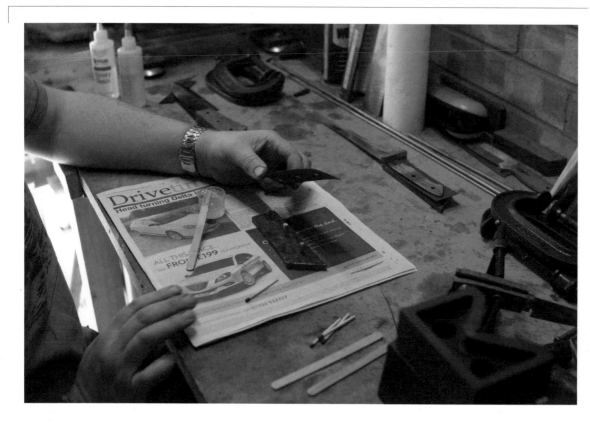

HOCKLEY, UNITED KINGDOM

GREEN MAN KNIVES

Tim Chilcott works out of a small workshop in Essex, where he makes beautiful sheath knives for field sports and bushcraft, and a range of culinary knives in both carbon and stainless steel for private and commercial clients.

Chilcott came to knife making after a long and successful career in silversmithing. Having achieved workshop manager for a prestigious London silversmith and mastering the trade, he began his own business; designing and producing bespoke items of domestic, ecclesiastic, ceremonial and civic silver. Disillusioned with the industry, however, due to the rising price of materials, and with much of his business being sourced from the Middle East during a difficult period in global politics, Chilcott became a teacher of Design Technology; but not before working on the largest piece of silverware ever made—a richly and ornately decorated 900 kg cake stand!

Having met a knife maker who was working in his department as a technician, Chilcott was encouraged to make his first knife. Today, he makes his knives through the method of "stock removal"—knives are produced from chunks of tool steel, which are first cut to shape, and then have their bevels (the surfaces that make the knife's cutting edge) ground down. Once the holes have been drilled for the handle fastenings, the metal, by now a knife 'blank', is heat treated to achieve the desired strength. When he has removed his knife blanks from his kiln, he can finish the blade to a razor sharp finish and fit the 'scales', or handle pieces. Chilcott uses a variety of exotic hardwoods for his handle materials, the desirable quality being extreme stability—woods that will not change shape, expand or contract as they take on and excrete moisture.

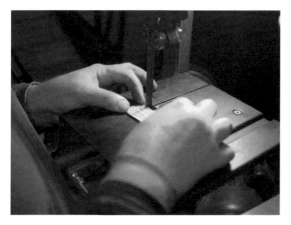

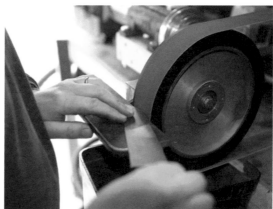

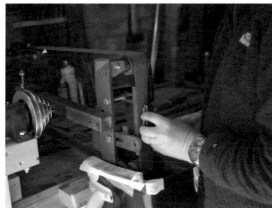

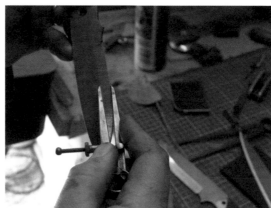

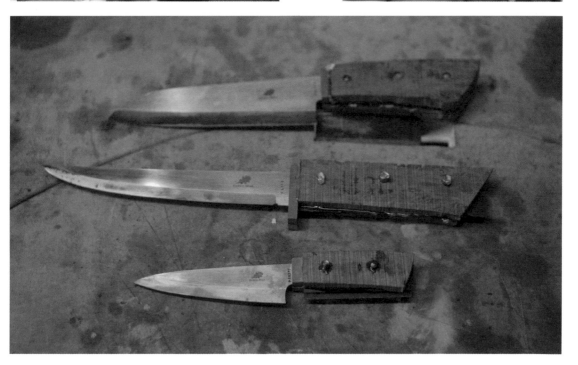

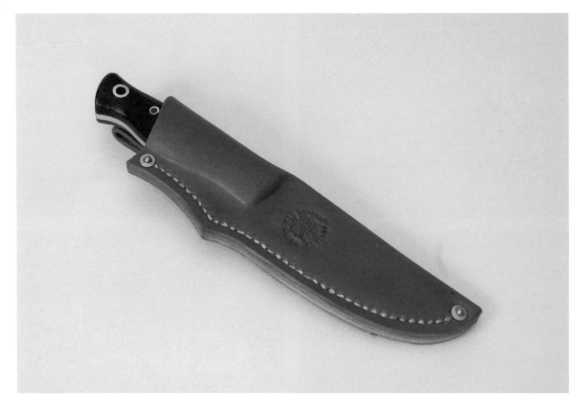

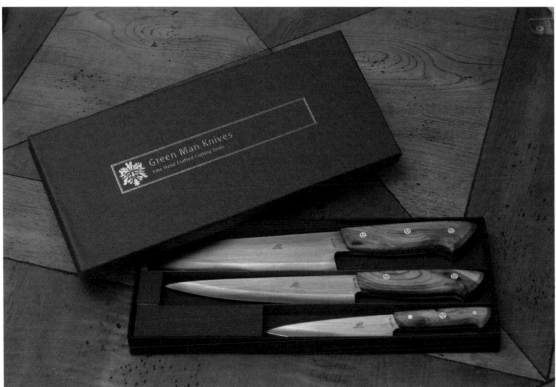

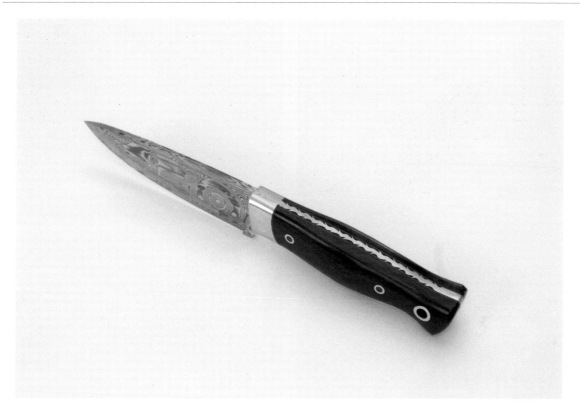

"Whilst teaching I met a young man who is a knife maker and he encouraged me to have a go. I find knives fascinating being such an ancient and fundamental tool."

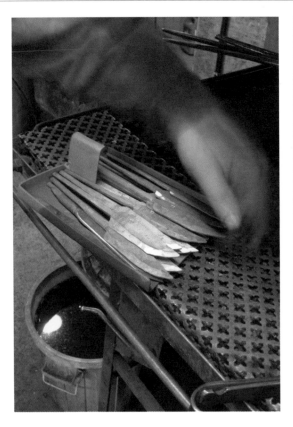
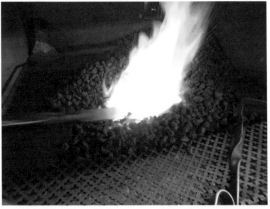
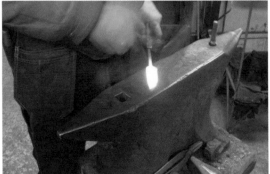

S DJÄRV HANTVERK AB

Sweden is a country well known for its excellent steel, and specifically its tool making. Svante and Elsa Djärv are a couple that live in rural Sweden and make wood working tools for a living, as they have been since the late 1980s. Perhaps most popular for their carving knives, the couple also make chisels and gouges to be used with lathes, axes and adzes and other wood working tools.

Svante, who makes the blades, does so by traditional Swedish methods that have not changed for hundreds of years. Heating steel to exact softness and then hammering them vigorously into shape he achieves, in his workshop, a blade of extremely high quality that still has a certain elegant crudeness to its form. The tools Svante makes are supplied razor sharp, and are forged so perfectly that they will last you a life time, being the ultimate blend of hardness, giving edge retention and durability, and softness, giving the blade a flexibility and avoiding a brittle edge, but also allowing the user to sharpen the tool easily. Part of the appeal of these tools is that they are made to be used; each tool differing slightly due to the rigorous beating the maker gives the steel. The marks of the maker remain with the tool throughout its life—these are not ornamental knives made to sit behind glass.

Elsa, Svante's business and life partner, is responsible for the manufacture of the tools' handles. Only the finest Swedish hardwoods are used, including Elm and Ash, grown in the county's south, and lumbered by a sawmill personally known to the Djärvs.

"We have a carving tradition all the way back to the Viking era. The edge is very sharp and keeps very sharp for a very long time. Around ten times longer than a mass-produced knife."

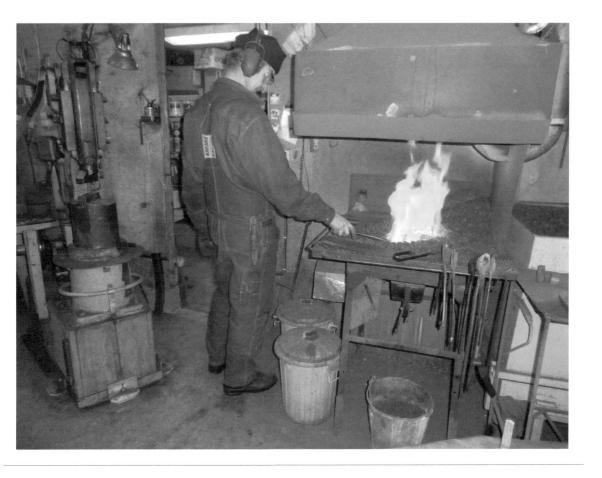

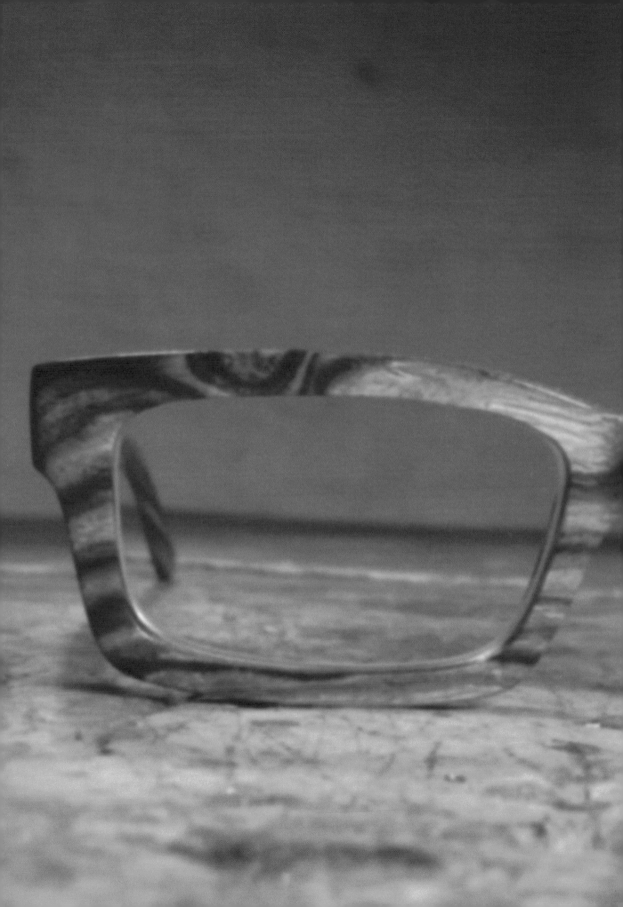

THE
SPECTACLE
MAKER

"I came of age in the 1990s, the era of plastic throw-aways. So it's no wonder that when I felt the weight in my hands of an object from some bygone era I saw the pride the creator put into making it as unique and special."

CHICAGO, UNITED STATES

URBAN SPECTACLES

The producers of handmade, wooden glasses, Urban Spectacles was fortuitously founded when, finding he could no longer glue together his dad's 1960s hand-me-down frames, Scott Urban recreated their parts from a solid chunk of wood with some DIY tools and sandpaper, scrambling them together with the old hinges and lenses. The homemade replacement pair worked surprisingly well—they looked good and people liked them because they were unusual—and making wooden specs became a new hobby, eventually leading him to a Brooklyn craft fair from which he gathered a handful of commissioning clients.

And it is still from commissions that Urban Spectacles operates today. Urban works closely with clients to create totally bespoke glasses; sometimes adapting a specific design they've worn or loved for years; sometimes getting to know them, their lives and their spectacle needs, and designing from scratch; all within the framework of his unique style and a high quality standards. The weight, fit, thickness and durability are all tailored perfectly to each individual, and this, along with the natural grain and texture of the wood, makes for totally custom, individual products.

Crafting the frames is an intense process that can take anything up to two years. During their production,

Urban 'lives with' each pair, perfecting them with his own self-taught techniques that, though perhaps somewhat unorthodox, contribute to their distinctive character. Instead of bending material to form curves, for example, he creates these directly in shaping from a larger block of material—a method he finds produces more naturally stable and better looking final products (though he admits this is a lesson he learnt from the rather less appealing results of unsuccessful experimentation in steam-bending wooden frames). Similarly, where mass-produced frames are typically finished in a machine, Urban's are all hand-sanded—a quality aspect of production he is proud of: "To me, where my work really shines and is alone is in the finishing process where care is taken and my hands are dirty—and all that dust is probably finding its way into my nose and lungs."

The bonds that Urban forms with all of his specs are reflected in those he makes with each of his patrons, for whom all the precision and attention is really put in. With every client, Urban Spectacles forms a friendship that lasts long after the job is complete: "The people I have made frames for so far are all very special people who for some reason believe in me. And when I meet them and spend time with them, that is far better than anything that I will make for them. It's a close second though."

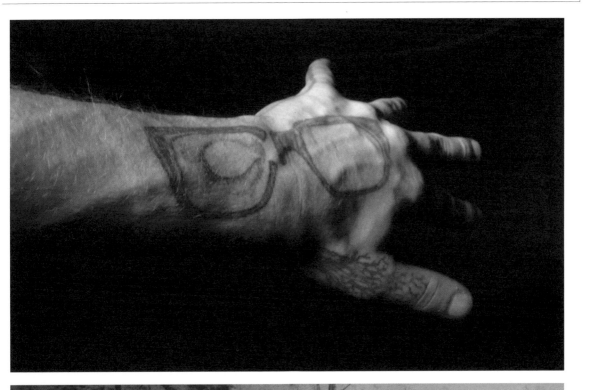

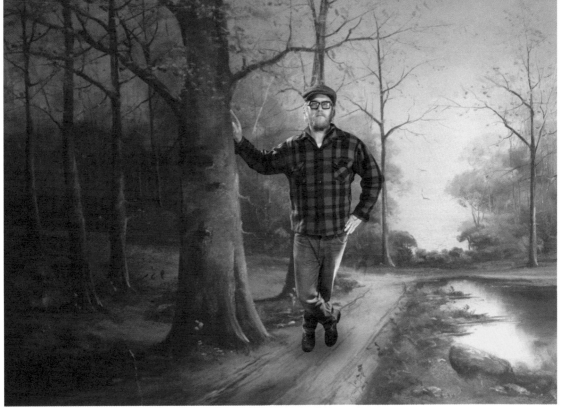

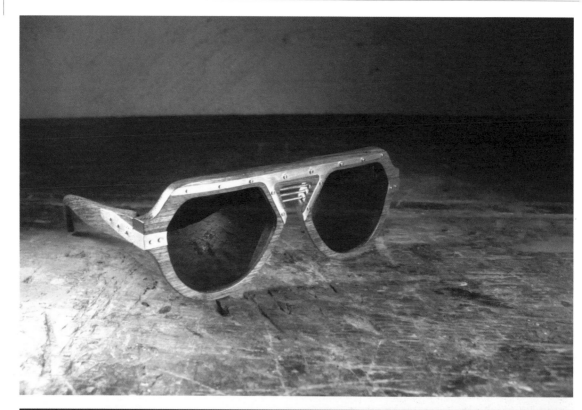

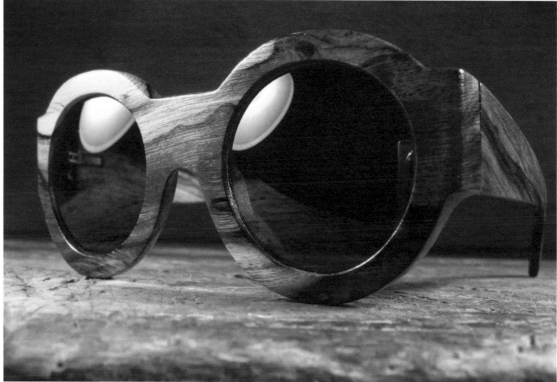

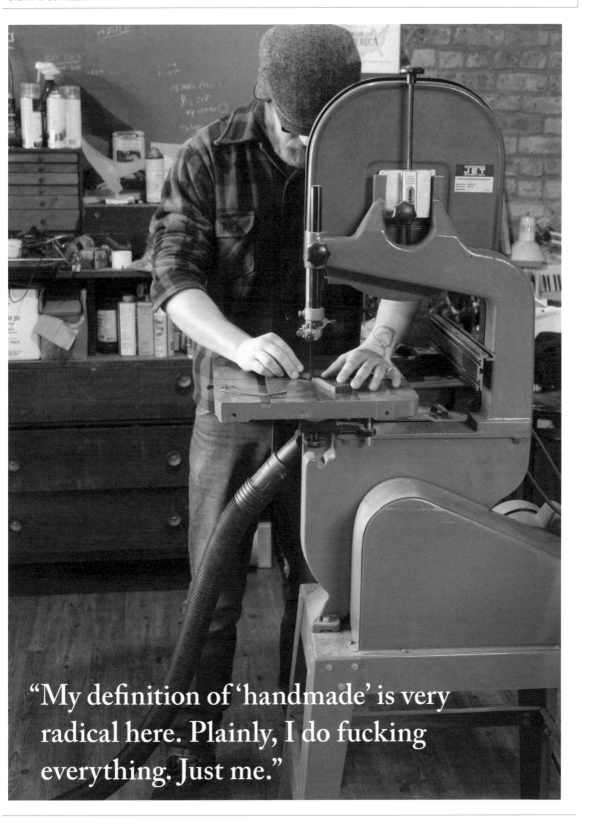

"My definition of 'handmade' is very radical here. Plainly, I do fucking everything. Just me."

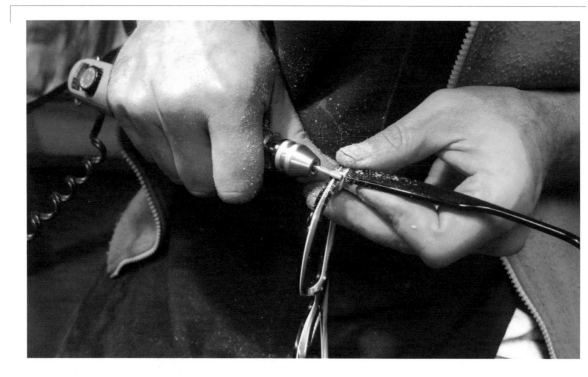

"Wearing Vinylize is a statement about a person's belief in sustainability. It serves as a reminder about the importance of environmentalism, durability and quality."

BUDAPEST, HUNGARY

VINYLIZE

That records can be played and listened to decades after their release is testimony to vinyl's surprising durability. Brothers Zachary and Zoltan, improvising with a box of their dad's old records which had been left aside in their workshop, thought of a way of applying this inherent longevity to useful, stylish and well made products. Vinylize make eyewear (as well as spectacle cases, display stands, lamp shades and bowls) out of recycled vinyl records—originally old Communist records found by trawling through Hungarian flea markets, but now sourced from out-of-business distributors with dead stock to shift.

Vinylize's products are distinctive and recognisable—the grain and grooves of the records remain visible on the frames, each of which are individually made by Tipton Eyewear in Budapest. The perceptible recycled material isn't just a stylistic consideration though, it's also evidence of the core belief in sustainability within Vinylize's practice.

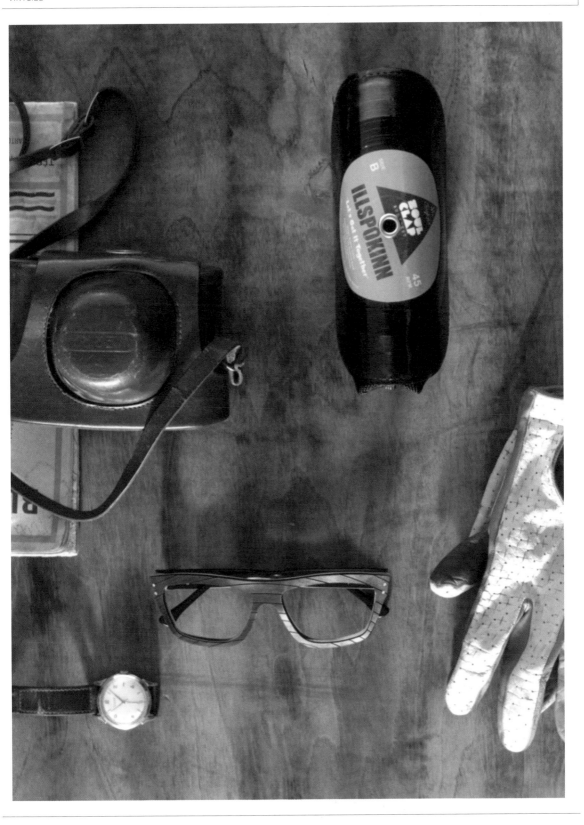

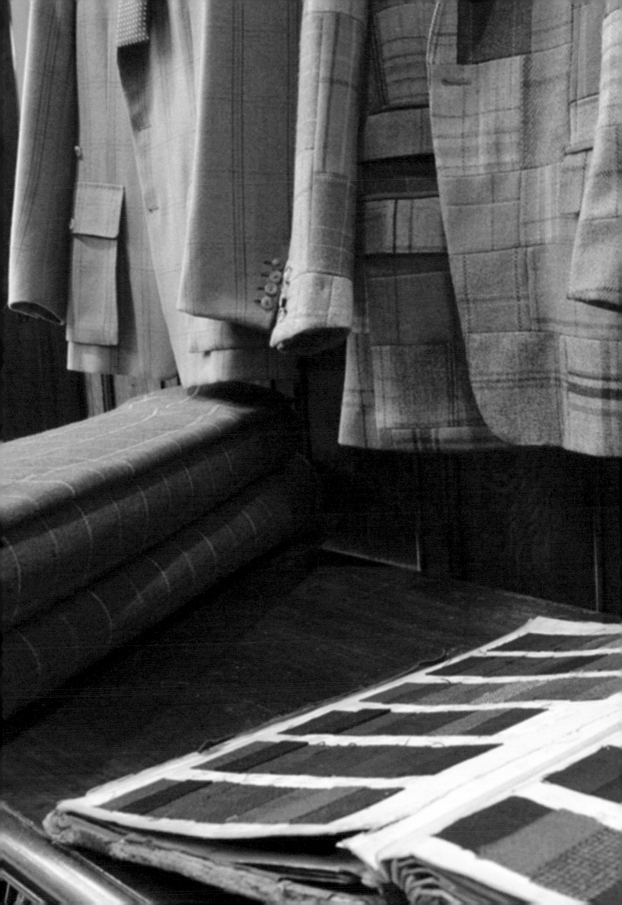

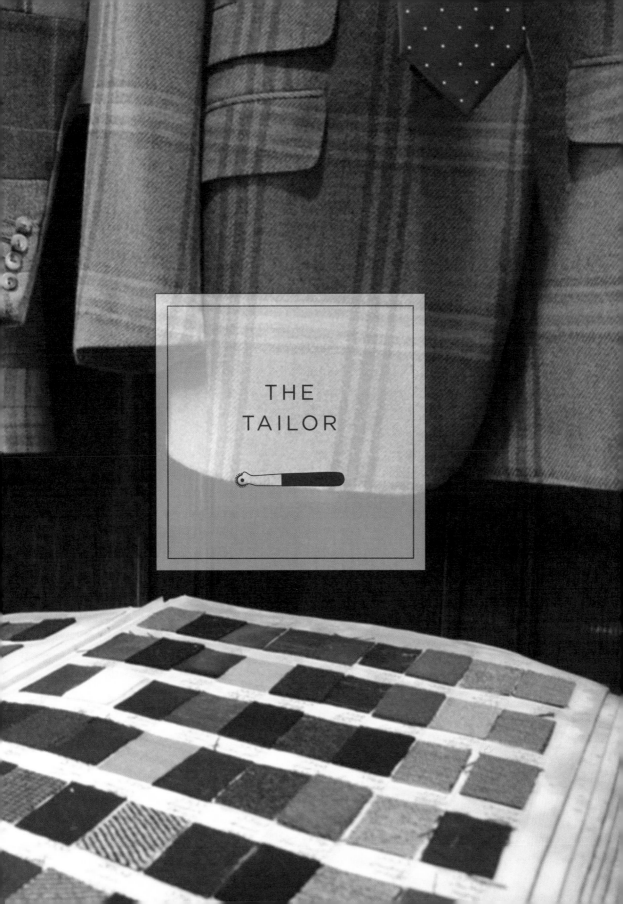

THE
TAILOR

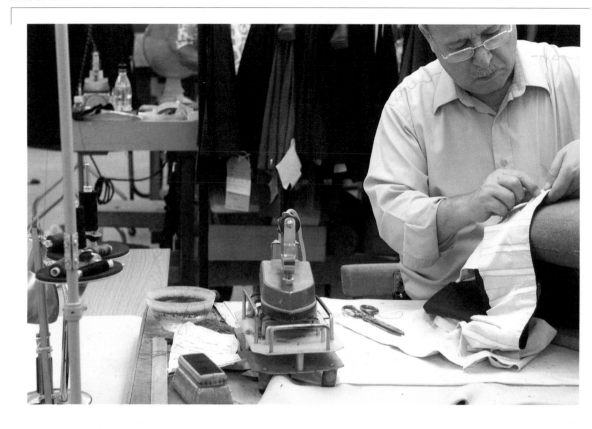

LONDON, UNITED KINGDOM

H HUNTSMAN & SONS

Bespoke handmade suits, in comparison to their off the peg counterparts, provide wearers with several things: a long lasting product, a perfect fit and an equally unique experience.

H Huntsman & Sons is a Savile Row tailors, founded in 1849 by Henry Huntsman, who still use meticulous, traditional tailoring techniques that are hundreds of years old. While, like each Savile Row tailor, H Huntsman & Sons have a distinct style—they make "a close fitting, very British suit with a firm shoulder"— every miniscule aspect of their custom made ensembles is designed and crafted with the wearer in mind.

There is a romanticism embroiled in owning and wearing a tailored suit, perhaps in part due to getting to know the person who makes it, and the knowledge that your item was made especially for you by such a highly skilled craftsman (at H Huntsman & Sons, training to become a tailor takes between at least five and six years, which is usually done in-house). Perhaps it results from the whole experience of having the suit made. At H Huntsman & Sons the process of tailoring a suit takes over 85 hours to complete and includes being assigned a personal, dedicated cutter, who carries out all of your fittings and is the "handwriting" behind your item, as well as specific coat and trouser makers to create the separate pieces—all of whom are not only appointed to you for one project, but also for any future orders with the company. Usually three fittings are required over a period of about ten weeks, in which your personal pattern is drawn and altered each time, eventually leaving you with a perfectly personalised garment.

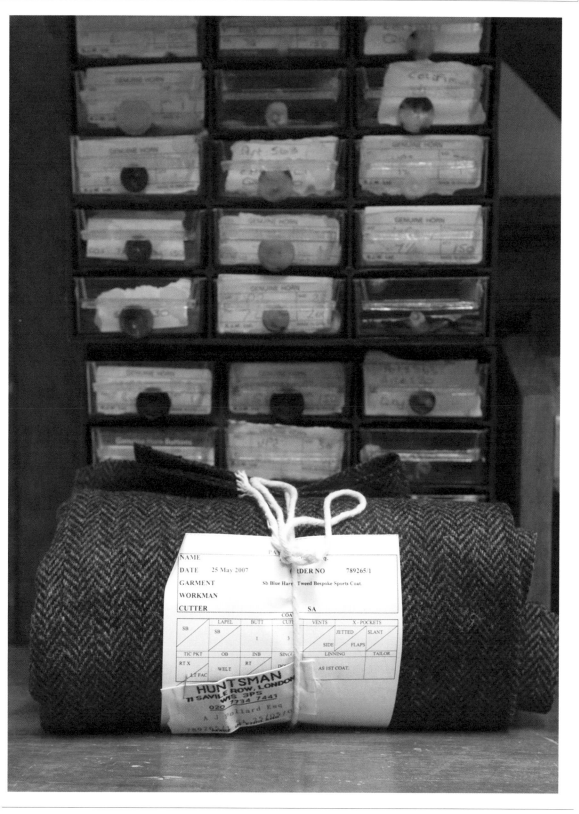

"A bespoke suit is a piece of engineering that sculpts the body, fits beautifully and feels fantastic on."

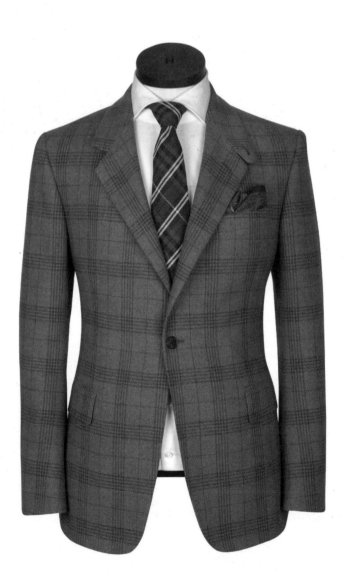

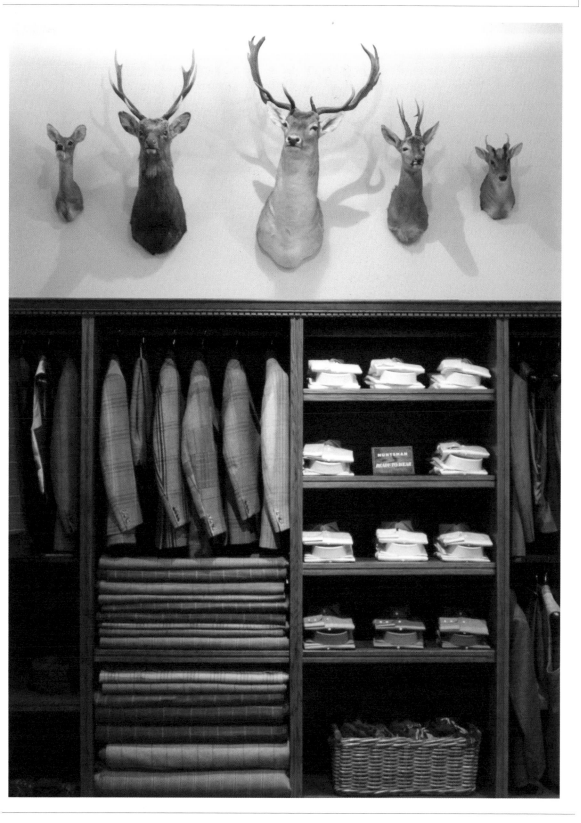

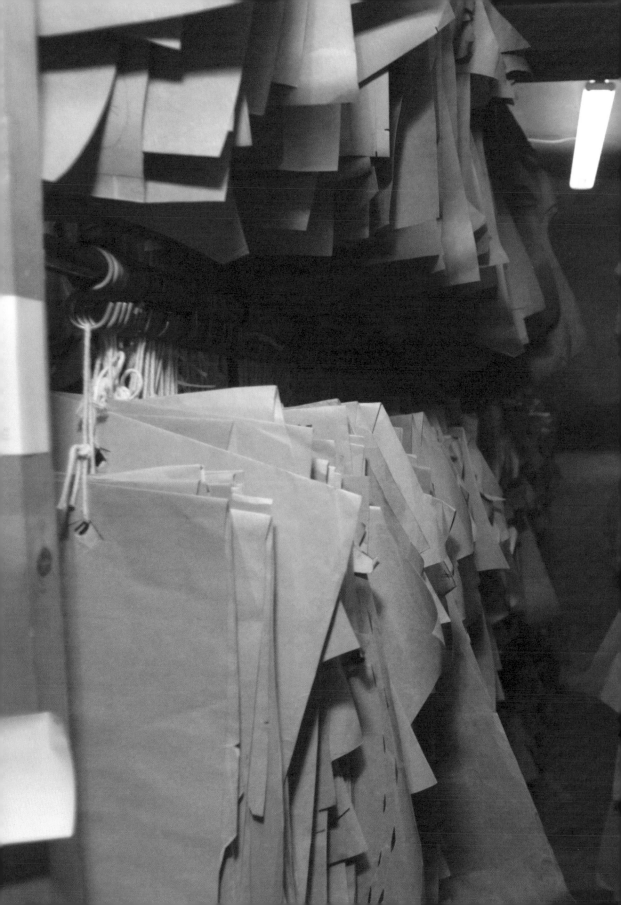

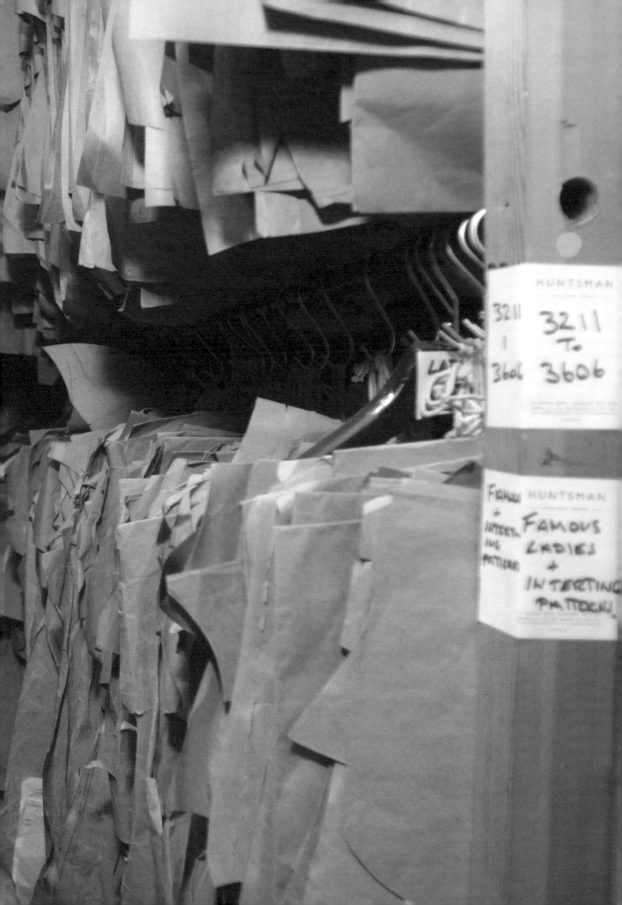

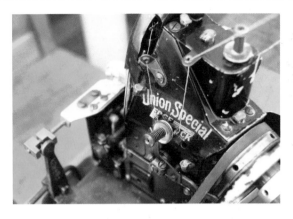 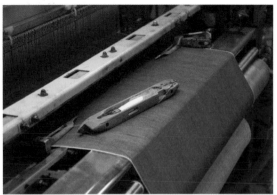

"There are many handmade items in Japan. This is a wonderful thing and I am proud of it."

OKAYAMA, JAPAN

MOMOTARO JEANS

Okayama-based Momotaro Jeans have been making a top quality, handmade alternative to mass-produced jeans since it was founded by Hisao Manabe in 2006.

Designed with a focus on the conventionally long-term use of jeans, and the wear and fading that happens as a result, Momotaro's products are crafted in every aspect. Their own signature denim alone can take up to three months to be produced, part of which consists of weaving the material on a loom with a technician on hand to listen to the rhythmic sounds and feel the fabric intermittently, monitoring the material's quality. After the denim is ready to use, it's a further one to two months before the jeans themselves are shaped and formed, but, as Momotaro insist, jeans that are worn and loved for a long time take a long time to craft. In fact, Momotaro Jeans' collection's most exclusive pairs are handmade with hand woven material that has been hand dyed in natural indigo, of which only 20 pairs a year are created.

For Momotaro Jeans, who are witnesses to a Japanese resurgence in craft amongst younger generations, the culture of the handmade is internationally important; they believe that while recent markets are increasingly digitalised and run with high-tech machinery, there remains within us an underlying love for the 'analogue' and the human touch. As Momotaro Jeans hope, each of their products "has spirit, craftsmanship and human kindness inside".

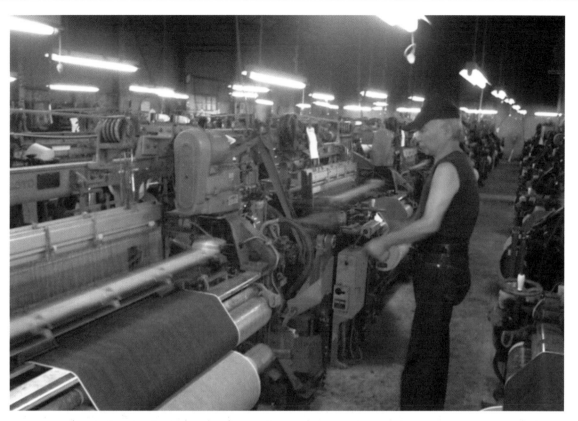

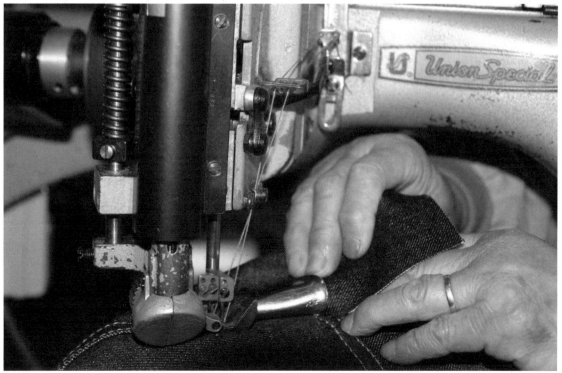

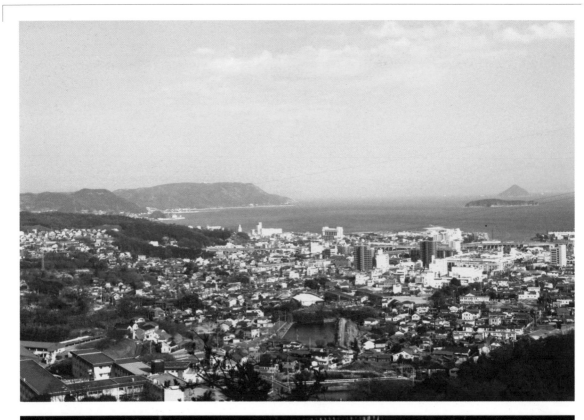

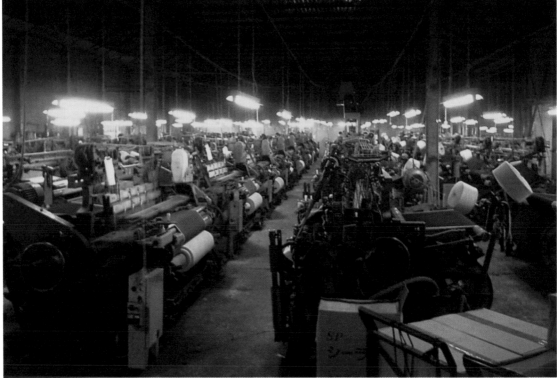

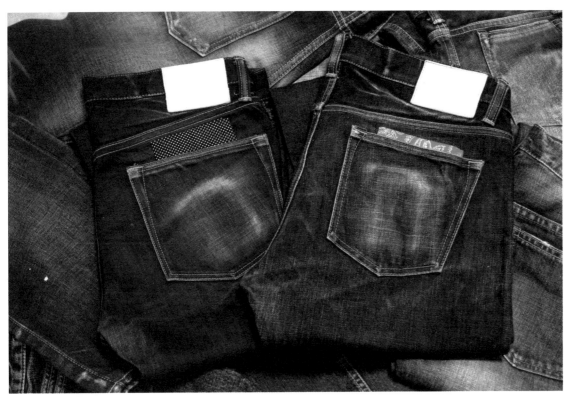

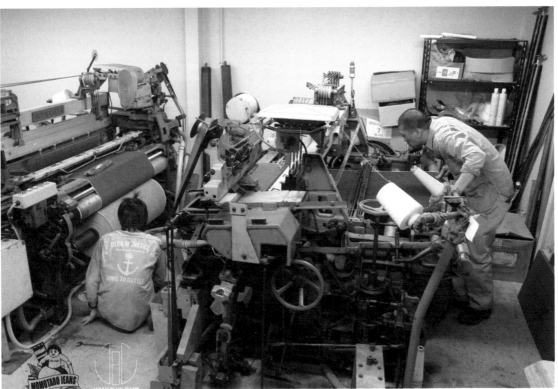

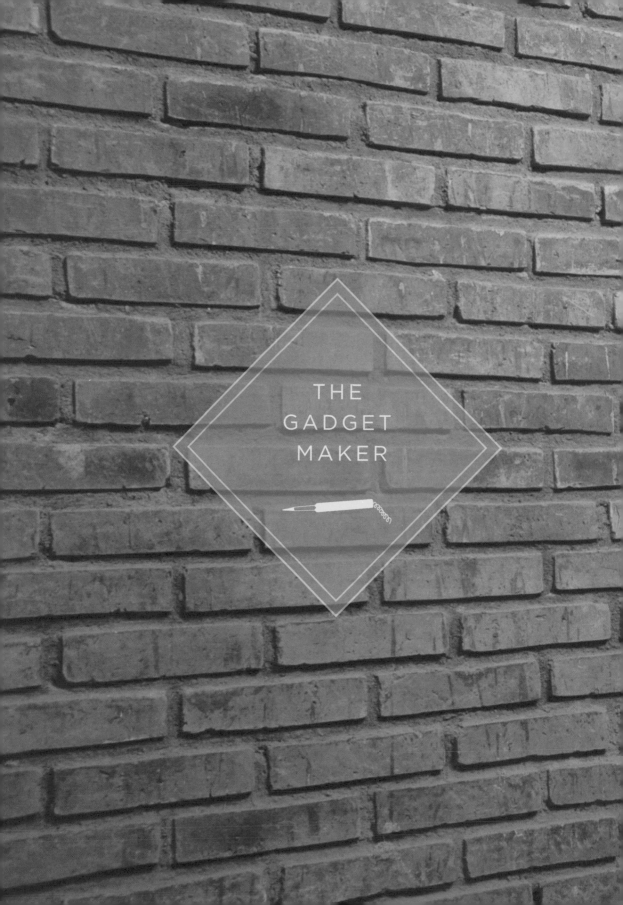

THE
GADGET
MAKER

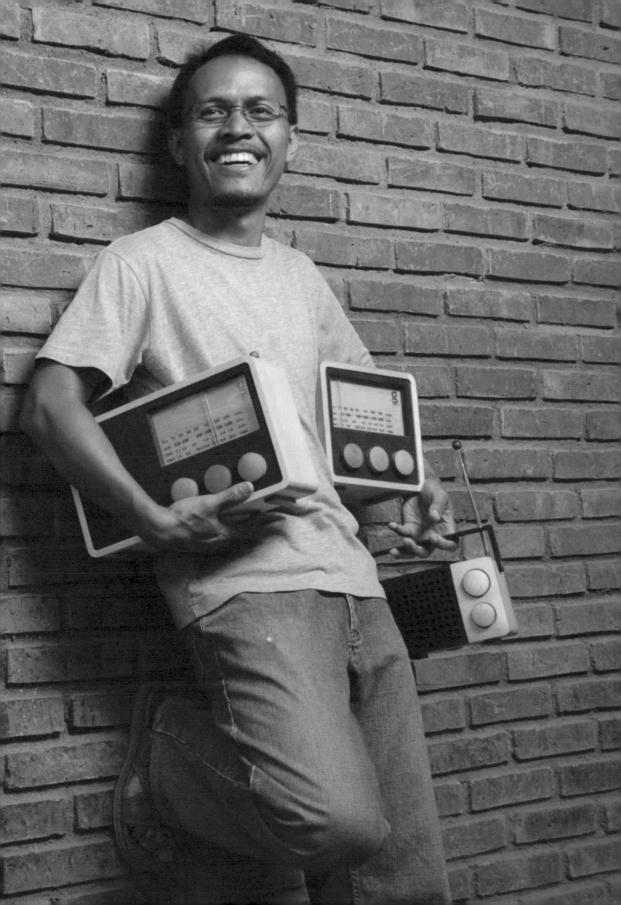

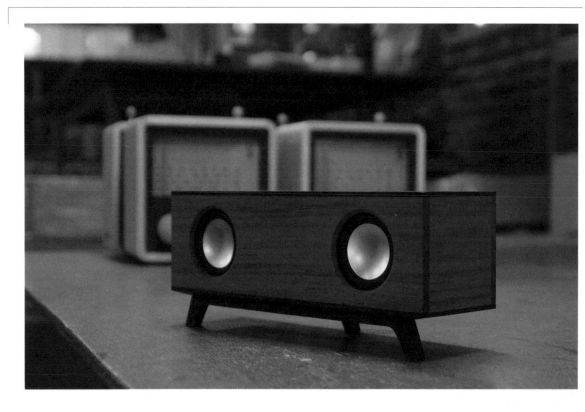

JAVA, INDONESIA

MAGNO

Magno was set up by product design graduate Singgih Kartono as an endeavour to replenish his Indonesian hometown community and make a business with as much care for the environment as for profit.

Governmental changes to agriculture in the area saw the deterioration of age-old farming traditions in Kandangan, Central Java, and ultimately the slowing down of village life and an increase in desperate, unecological money making practices in the surrounding countryside. Having grown up in the area, which is rich with natural materials including various types of wood, Kartono had both a close relationship with and respect for nature, and an understanding of Indonesia's traditional crafts. Combining the two, he designed products—such as his internationally acclaimed radio—handmade in the locally available wood resources by village-based employees. The resulting business is combating environmentally unethical practices in the local area—since their beginnings Magno has planted and nursed more than twice the hectares of

woodland than it has used—whilst supporting people in the area and making sensible, fair use of the human resources too, a "weapon of survival" for the village.

This approach to product manufacture also allowed Kartono to produce authentic, handmade items, but to a standard quality—a modern means of managing traditional techniques that he calls "new craft". Nonetheless each individual is important in his operation—Magno won't exceed a certain number of craftsmen in case their name is reduced to a number—as are the handmade qualities in the products. Traces of the craftsman's handwork on a product are important to Kartono:"it feels soulful". And the character of a product is carried on into its life as a possession. Magno's products are only oiled, not coated. This means that they must be taken care of, something Kartono feels should be an integral part of the relationship we have with the things around us, and something which could go some way towards minimising the current culture of colossal consumption.

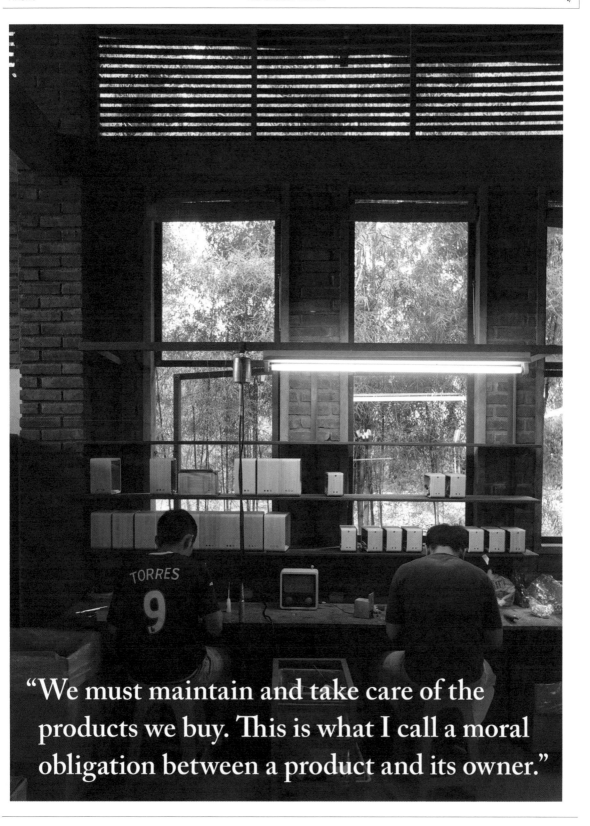

"We must maintain and take care of the products we buy. This is what I call a moral obligation between a product and its owner."

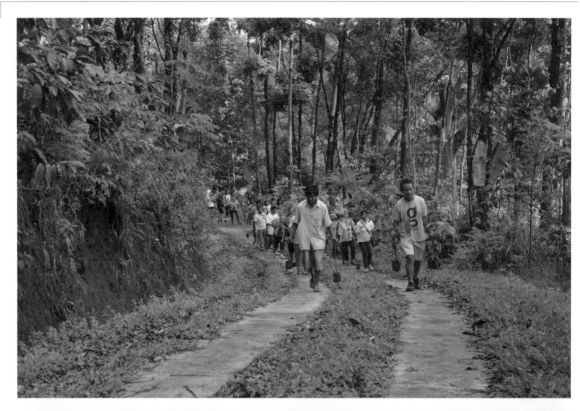

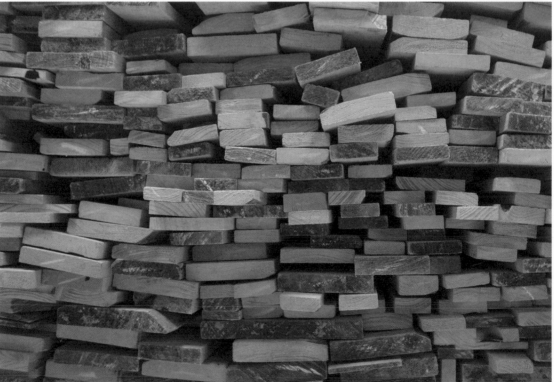

"What people do mostly disturbs the balance of nature. A weakness of being human is the difficulty to say 'enough'."

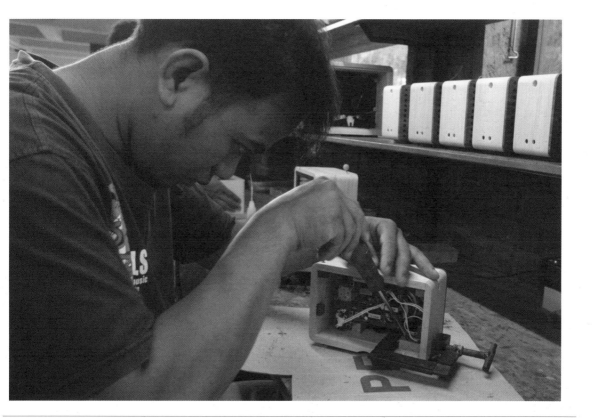

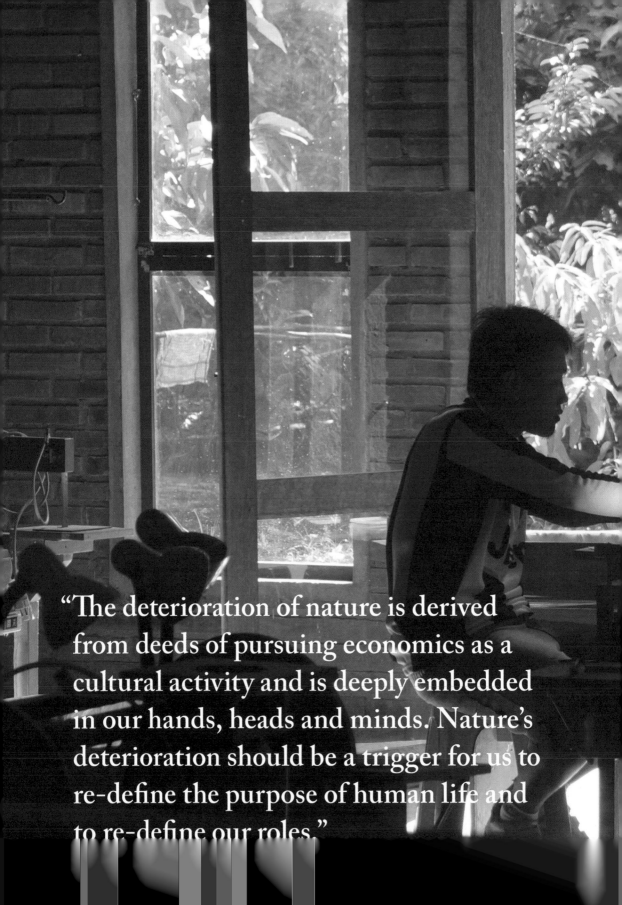

"The deterioration of nature is derived from deeds of pursuing economics as a cultural activity and is deeply embedded in our hands, heads and minds. Nature's deterioration should be a trigger for us to re-define the purpose of human life and to re-define our roles."

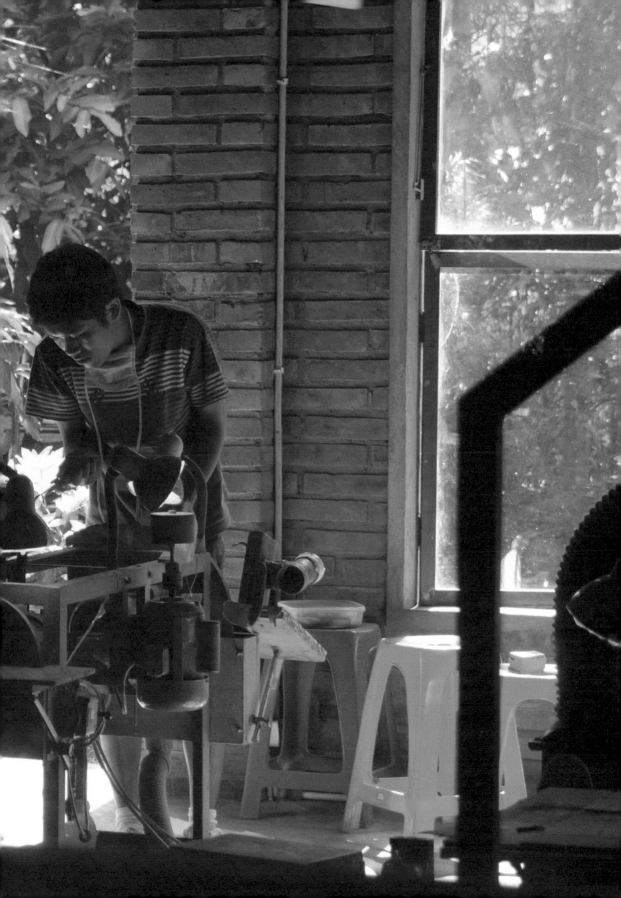

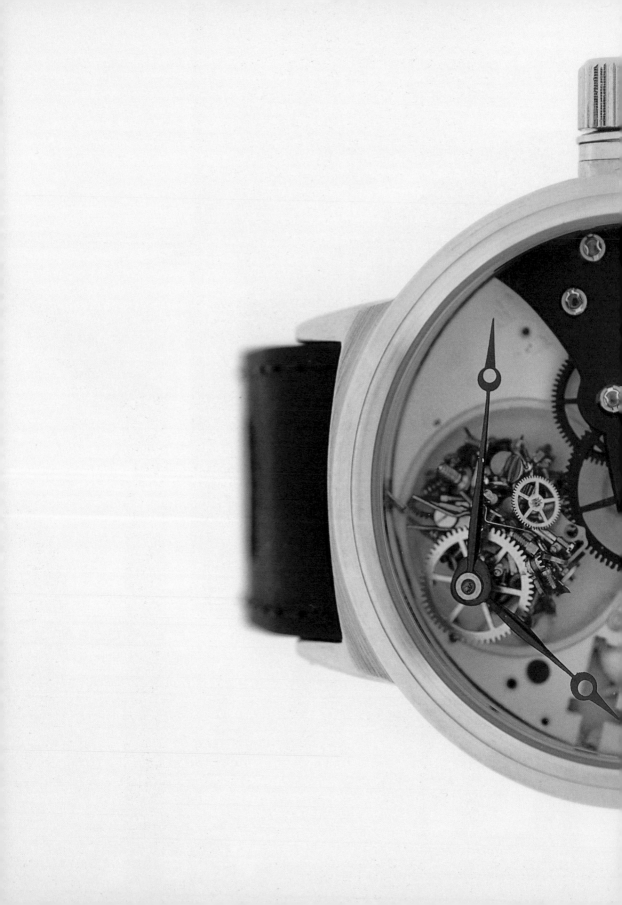

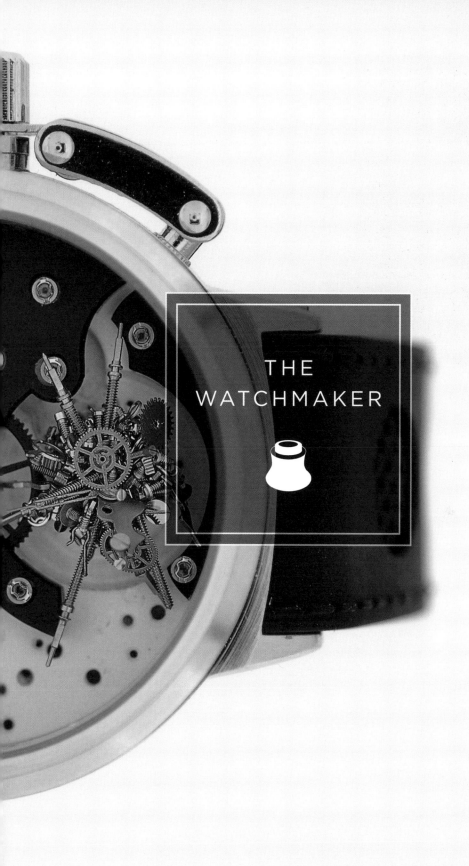

THE
WATCHMAKER

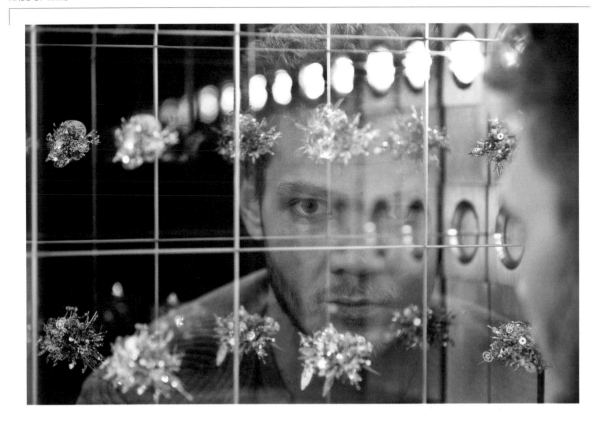

QUENTIN CARNAILLE

Quentin Carnaille makes "wearable sculptures" with working watch movements. Experiments in changing the way we understand time and perceive its passing, Carnaille's watches are far from the conventional timepiece. Fascinated by infinity, relativity, astronomy and the origin of time reading, he makes "timekeepers" that don't actually tell the time. He describes his watches as questioning our relationship with time and the eternal, just as the ruins of Mayan civilisation or the Parthenon in Athens remain extraordinarily beautiful despite having lost their original vocations.

Having first trained as an architect, Carnaille was inspired to pursue his interest in the relationship between watchmaking and time after creating a pair of cufflinks out of some found 1930s watch components—a gift he gave his father. He has since continued to create his pieces with only the finest old movements dating from the same period or earlier; these raw materials are what inspire the design and meticulous hand creation of each piece. Machines, Carnaille emphasises, couldn't make his timekeepers. The beauty of their being handmade lies also in the fact that they are not a part of the wider commercial market or a scheme of mass consumption, but an utterly unique item.

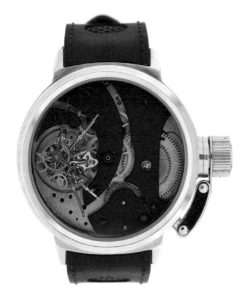

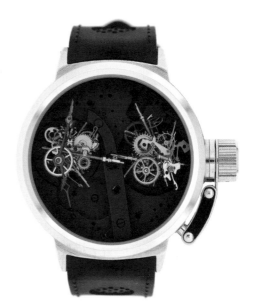

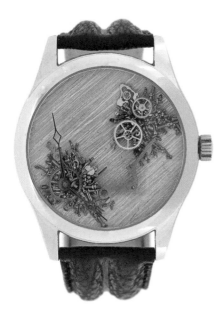

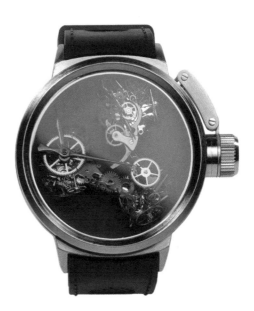

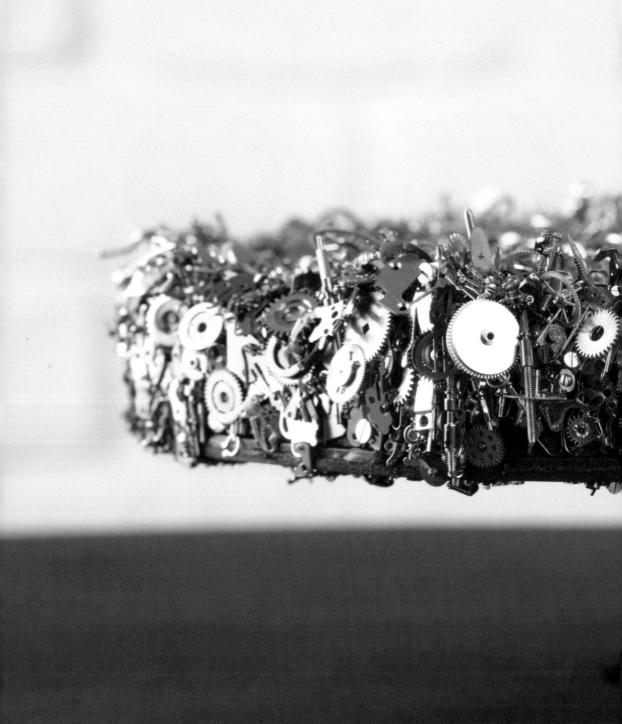

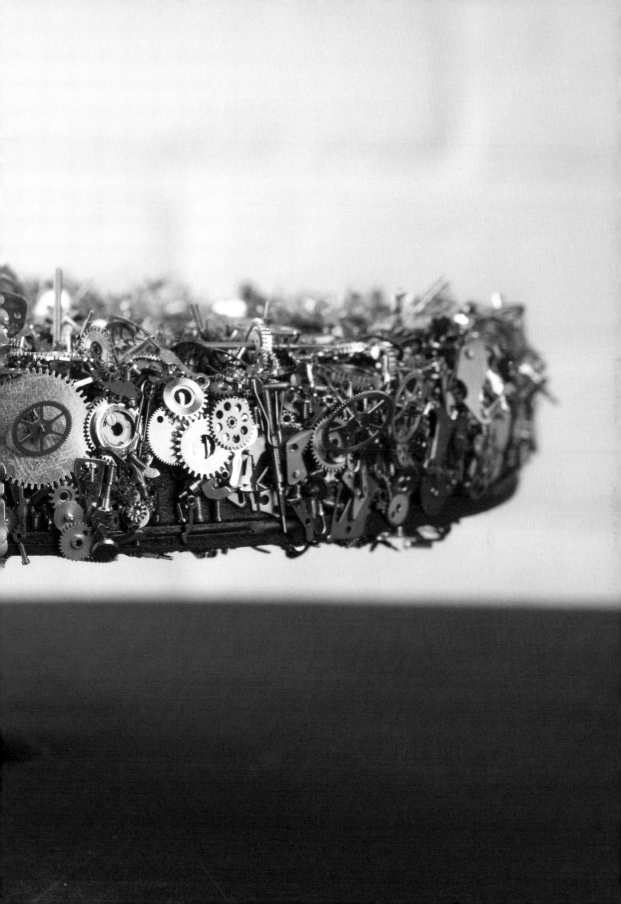

"Every industry needs its niche rebels to evolve."

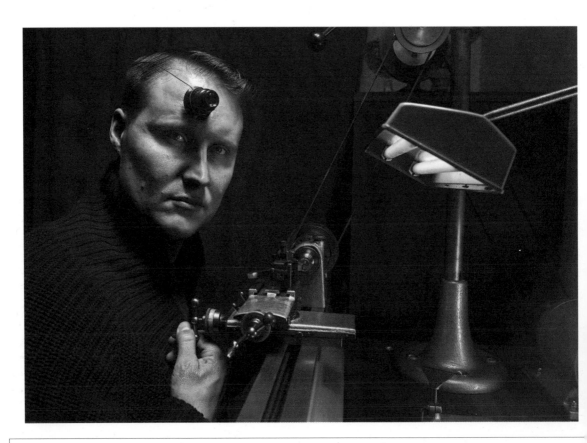

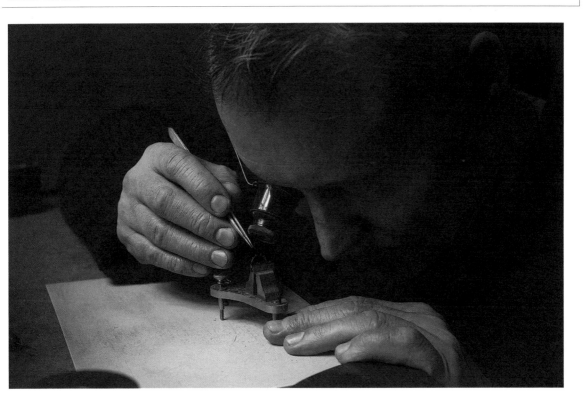

RÖNKKÖ WATCHES

The by-line of Rönkkö Watches reads "handmade in Finnish silence", and silence certainly is an integral factor of the practice, according to owner and watchmaker Antti Rönkkö. In Finland, he explains, silence is rooted in the appreciation of others, the time for thoughts and reflections, and "creating something out of nothing"; in the silence of the night while everyone else sleeps, Antti creates.

A lifelong interest in the intricate mechanics of watches led Rönkkö to study at the Tapiola School of Watchmaking and, while he held a position for over a decade in Nokia's research centre designing and prototyping mechanical components such as delicate hinges and slides, he moonlighted as watchmaker at his own bench, until finally he was able to focus solely on his own business.

Inspired by ancient Greek myths—stories about being human—Rönkkö Watches are designed to help their wearers gain a little self-knowledge, "if they're willing to do a bit of soul-searching". The Steel Labyrinth design, for example, is adorned with an intertwining maze pattern, a representation of the tool for contemplation, and aid to meditation and personal insight; the labyrinth—as Rönkkö calls it is a "personal pilgrimage".

Intimately handmade with the finest materials and movements that Rönkkö has himself taken years to design and perfect, Rönkkö Watches are of such high quality that he believes they will outlive their wearers, a thought that occurs to him in the "profoundly humbling moment" when still parts first spring to life. This longevity, he firmly states, is achieved because they are made by hand. His view of the distinction between handmade watches and their mass-produced counterparts? It's like "the difference between a respected unique piece of art and a blockbuster movie poster on your wall".

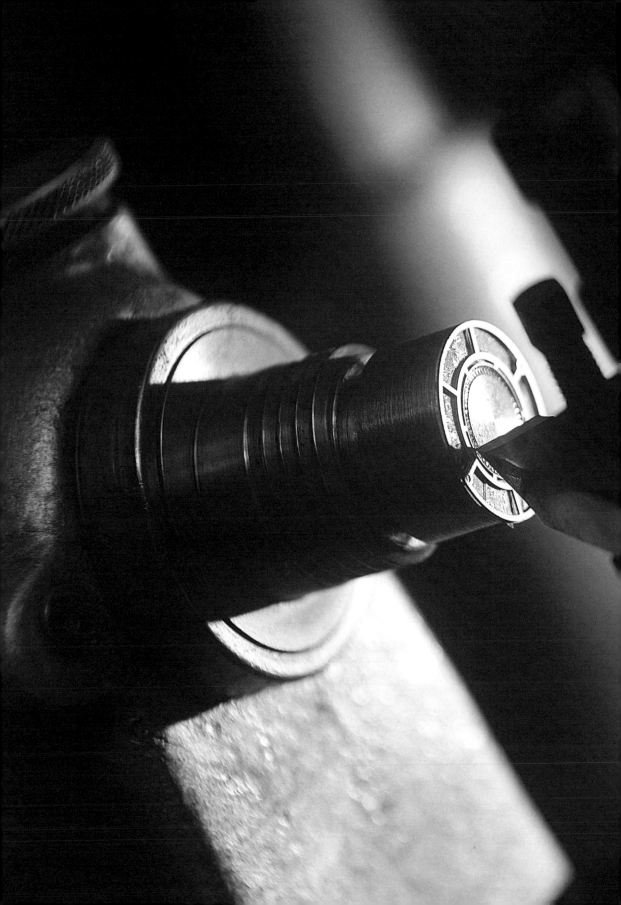

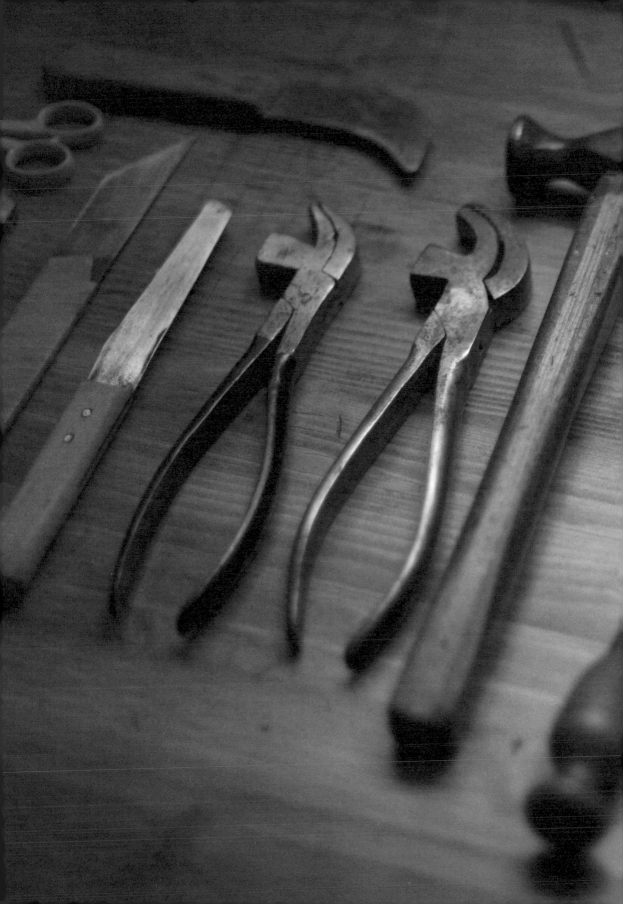

GLOSSARY
OF
TOOLS

COBBLER'S HAMMER

A cobbler's—or cordwainer's—hammer's idiosyncrasies appear via its enlarged, flattened striking surface, used to hammer and tap in hobnails, tacks and pegs, as well as flattening seams and tapping out creases in the leather upper during the lasting process; and the oddly curved pane end of the head, used for flattening leather, pressing the outsole into the insole, or to press layers of leather in to each other.

CHAIN WHIP

The chain whip comprises a metal bar or handle with a length of bike chain. It is used as a wrench to remove threaded sprockets, or to stop sprockets freewheeling when removing a lock ring.

NEON BULB

A regular bulb consists of a glass bowl containing a filament through which an electric charge is passed, resulting in light as the wire heats up. A neon bulb is filled with neon gas, which glows or fluoresces when an electric charge is passed through it. A transformer and capacitor build up this charge, which moves through gas around 60 times a second.

THREAD SNIPS

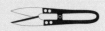

Thread snips are typically short-bladed, pivoted or sprung shears, rendered sharper so as to cleanly cut rather than tear material. When pivoted by way of a screw holding the unit together, they tend to have a single integrated finger hole.

BAMBOO SPLITTER

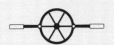

A rudimentary but effective tool, a bamboo splitter is used to break bamboo into equal shaped strands. The circular face of the splitter is placed on the cut shoot, and hammered with a maul to start the split. It is then pushed through the entire shoot with the attached handles.

WEAVING SHUTTLE

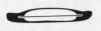

A tool used in the construction of textiles, a shuttle contains the weft thread that is drawn through the vertical warp yarns to build up the body of a weave. A rudimentary shuttle simply comprises a single piece of wood with notches in which to wrap the yarn, whilst more complex examples factor elements such as rotating bobbins to more swiftly deploy yarn through the warp.

ENGLISH WOOL COMB

A traditional wood comb takes the form of a wooden handle and base embedded with a number of metal spikes or "tines". Two combs are used to refine the matted wool. The cut end of the wool is pushed down on to the tines of one comb; the second comb is then pulled across the uncut ends of the woollen "beard", unmatting the wool and transferring it to this second comb. When this process is complete, the wool can be drawn through a disc called a "diz" ready for spinning.

PURFLING PICK

The purfling pick is a very small, narrow-bladed chisel used in the delicate process of inlaying a decorative wood detail around the edge of stringed instruments including the violin, cello and double bass. A purfling marker scores two parallel lines around the instrument, which are then deepened with a knife. The purfling pick is used to remove the wood between the two lines to form a purfling channel into which the inlay is inserted.

DIAMOND SHEARS

Diamond sheers are tools used in glasswork and glassblowing. They are often multi-use: the diamond-shaped hole between the blades is designed specifically for cutting circular objects, though blunt edges are occasionally built in with which to pick up and move pipes and punties (iron rods used to shape soft glass).

SUKETA

A *suketa* is a tool used in the making of handmade paper. It comprises two separate parts: the *su* is a split-bamboo screen cover; the *keta* the large wooden frame that the cover fits in to by way of hinges, and which is traditionally constructed of Japanese cyprus.

QUOIN KEY

In letterpressing, a quoin is a metal or wooden wedge used to lock type, leading, and furniture into the frame or chase. When set, this is known as the "form". So-called "hi-speed" quoins are now more commonly used than the traditional wedge, applying an equal force horizontally across the quoin face. A quoin key is the tool used to tighten the quoin in the chase.

AWL

An awl is a simple tool for punching holes in material and leather, as well as sewing heavy materials. It comprises a rounded wooden handle with a sharp, thick metal needle, either straight or with a curved end. In effect, they function as inverted needles for sewing, with the thread hole located at the pointed end of the metal shaft. They are used across many disciplines, such as leatherwork, shoemaking and bookbinding.

PLANE

A plane is a tool used to flatten, strip and smooth wood. Manual hand planes generally comprise a cutting edge—usually a metal plate—attached to a body block, which is pushed—only Japanese planes are pulled—over the wood to strip consistent shavings until the surface is levelled. The fundamental design of the hand plane is particularly ancient, originating thousands of years ago.

-CLAMP

G- or C-clamps are rudimentary clamping tools, usually constructed of steel or cast iron, and so-called due to their resemblance —with or without their fundamental screw component—to the alphabetical letters.

NI ROTARY SANDER

The rotary sander is a circular electric sander, commonly used in carpentry to smooth down rough wood and create curved surfaces. In the instance of tie making, a miniature form is used to tend to the small surfaces of material and intricate ersatz crinkles of the tie form.

ALETTE KNIFE

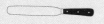

A flat, flexible and usually blunt tool, the palette knife—the name derived from the traditional artist's tool—is commonly used to mix paints and pastes, and to create marbling effects for book endpapers and suchlike.

ESSENTIAL OILS BOTTLES

Essential oil containers are idiosyncratically stout glass bottles, usually with screw lids. These oils are relatively volatile, and often prone to damage by heat and oxidisation. For this reason, oil bottles were historically of a dark amber colour, as this helped to filter out the sun's ultra-violet rays. Though often still of a dark hue, contemporary bottles are commonly found in purple, green and blue colours as well as the traditional amber.

DIVIDING CALIPER

A calliper is a device used to read the distance between an objects two opposite sides. Though a dial calliper is commonly used to accurately measure distance to tiny measurements, a divider caliper (the single 'l' spelling being used to technically delineate a pair of callipers), more commonly known as a compass, can be set to a single measurement to check an evenly ground bevel during knife making.

BLACKSMITH'S HAMMER

A simple example of a hammer, the blacksmith's tool is commonly used with an anvil to flatten and shape heat-softened metal, primarily wrought-iron and steel. This process is called forging.

OPTICAL SCREWDRIVER

An optical screwdriver is a perfunctory kind of miniature tool, made to fit the atypically small screws seen on spectacles. They are often supplied with interchangeable flat and Phillips heads of differing sizes, and occasionally incorporate magnifying lenses to aid use.

PATTERN TRACING WHEEL

A tracing wheel is used in tailoring, and typically comprises a short handle with a rotating wheel for marking textile pattern designs on tracing paper. These designs are then transferred to material before cutting.

The wheel itself is either serrated or smooth, and dual-wheel examples can be used to mark out both design boundaries and seam allowances.

SOLDERING IRON

Usually comprising an insulated plastic handle with a metal a tip, a soldering iron is used to melt solder—a metal alloy—in order to fuse links between workpiece components. The metal tip is heated with

an electric charge, usually via a mains connection but occasionally by battery. They are commonly used in electronics manufacturing to build microchips and motherboards.

WATCHMAKER'S LOUPE

A loupe—or hand lens—is an integral tool in watchmaking, specifically in the assembly of mechanisms, the dial itself, and the insertion of decorative aesthetic elements such as precious stones within the face. The

focussing lens or lenses are self-contained within the cylindrical body of the loupe, occasionally with an attached housing in to which this can be folded for protection.

TUNING PEG

A tuning peg is a fundamental component of most stringed instruments. Usually attached to the headstock (such as with a violin or cello) though occasionally also to places such as the neck of an instrument (as on a five-string banjo), turning it relaxes or tightens

the string. Violin family instruments tend to have tapered pegs that can be pulled out slightly to loosen and pushed in to the headstock to tighten. The solid geared kind found on many guitars and derivatives are referred to as machine heads.

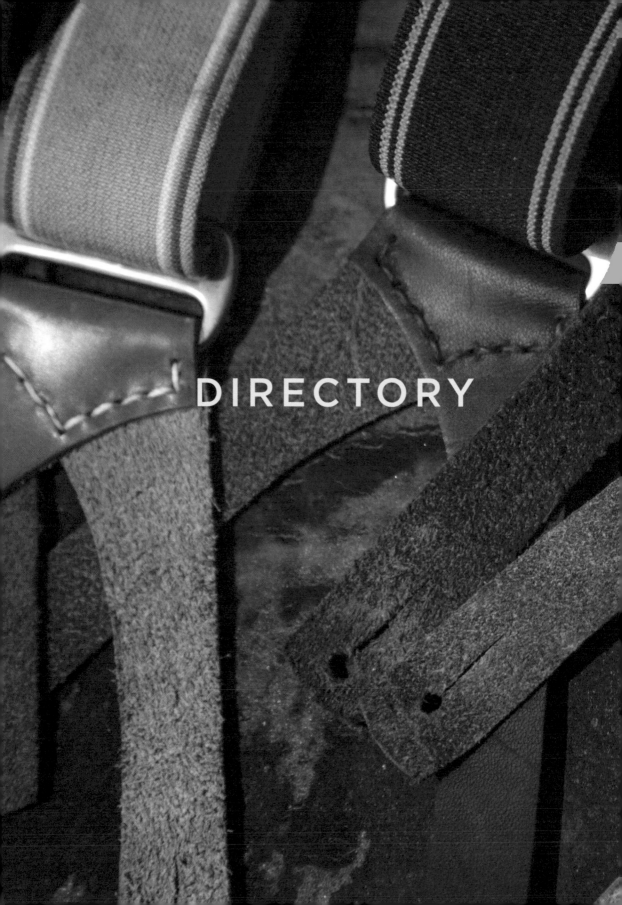

DIRECTORY

THE SHOEMAKER

Alexander Reed
Yew Tree Cottage
Stockwood Farm
Ellenwhorne Lane
Staple Cross
East Sussex
TN32 5RR, UK
www.alexreedshoes.com

Viktoria Nilsson
Norrbölegatan 37
Skellefteå, 93140, Sweden
www.viktorianilsson.se

Claire Best
87 Albert Street
East Brunswick, Australia
www.clairebest.com.au

THE BICYCLE BUILDER

Tom Donhou
www.donhoubicycles.com

St Joris Cycles
Sint Jorislaan 16
5611 PM Eindhoven
The Netherlands
www.stjoriscycles.nl

THE NEON SIGN MAKER

God's Own Junk Yard
Unite 12, Ravenswood
Industrial Estate
Shernhall Street
London E17 9HQ, UK
www.godsownjunkyard.co.uk

Artistic Neon
887 Cypress Avenue
Ridgewood, NY
11385, US
www.artisticneon.com

Todd Sanders
1720 S First Street
Austin, Texas
78704, US
www.roadhouserelics.com

THE BAG MAKER

Trakke
Trakke Basecamp
65 Haugh Road
Glasgow G3 8TX, UK
www.trakke.co.uk

John Cho Moore
www.johnchomoore.com

THE TEXTILE MAKER

Dashing Tweeds
26 Sackville Street
London W1S 3HE, UK
www.dashingtweeds.co.uk

Sheep of Steel
Studio 2, Ridley Road Studios
51-63 Ridley Road
London E8 2NP, UK
www.sheepofsteel.com

THE MUSICAL INSTRUMENT MAKER

Andreas Hudelmayer
Studio 11, Craft Central
21 Clerkenwell Green
London EC1R 0DX, UK
www.hudelmayer.com

Yuri Landman
www.hypercustom.com

Michael Rucci
www.handmadeelectronic
instruments.com

THE GLASSWORKER

Brooklyn Glass
103–14th Street Enter
142 13th Street Brooklyn
NY 11215, US
www.brooklynglass.com

Stewart Hearn
Stewart Hearn London
Glassworks
112a High Street
Chatteris, Cambridgeshire
PE16 6NN, UK
www.stewarthearn.com

Amanda Winfield
www.abinger-stained-glass.
co.uk

THE STATIONER

Awagami
136 Kawahigashi
Yamakawa-cho
Yoshinogawa-shi
Tokushima 779-3401, Japan
www.awagami.com

Serrote
www.serrote.com

Bomo Art
Régiposta utca 14
1052 Budapest, Hungary
www.bomoart.com

Michael O'Brien
7 Tyne Street
Oamaru 9400, New Zealand
www.bookbinder.co.nz

THE WOODWORKER

John Eadon
Napton Holt
Holt Road
Southam, Warwickshire
CV47 1AJ, UK
www.johneadon.co.uk

Nic Webb
www.nicwebb.com

THE SARTORIALIST

Brackish
www.brackishbowties.com

Ella Bing Bow Ties
www.ellabing.com

For Holding Up The Trousers
www.forholdingupthe-
trousers.tumblr.com

THE COSMETICIST

Honest Skincare
www.honestskincare.co.uk

THE BLADESMITH

**Green
Man Knives**
15 Belvedere Avenue
Hockley, Essex
SS5 4UL, UK
www.greenmanknives.com

S Djärv Hantverk AB
Sör Nävde 15
SE-774 92 Avesta , Sweden
www.djarv.se

Orchard Steel
orchardsteel@gmail.com

THE SPECTACLE MAKER

Urban Spectacles
www.urbanspectacles.com

THE TAILOR

H Huntsman & Sons
11 Savile Row
London W1S 3PS, UK
www.h-huntsman.com

Momotaro Jeans
4047-8, Ajino, Kojima
Kurashiki-Shi, Okayama
Japan
www.momotarojeans.net

THE GADGET MAKER

Magno
www.magno-design.com

THE WATCHMAKER

Rönkkö Watches
Kalakontintie 1 F 56
Espoo 02230, Finland
www.ronkkowatches.fi

Quentin Carnaille
62 Rue du Faubourg des
Postes
59000 Lille, France
contact@quintincarnaille.com

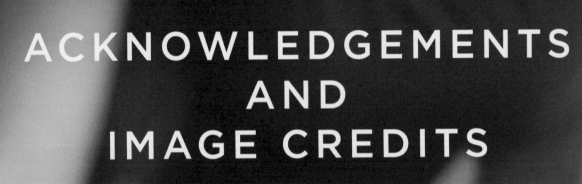

ACKNOWLEDGEMENTS
AND
IMAGE CREDITS

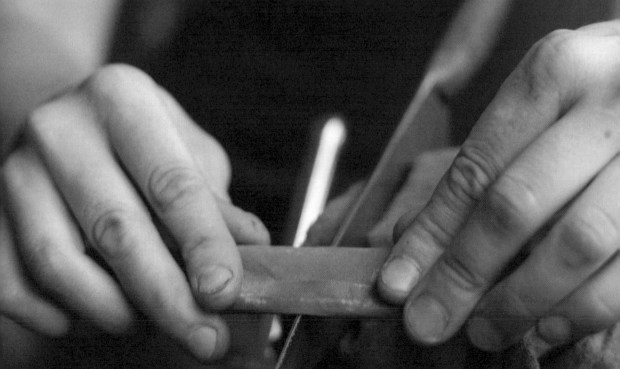

ACKNOWLEDGEMENTS

Many thanks to Amy Cooper-Wright for her hard work and vision in realising the book's design, and to João Mota and Sylvia Ugga for their creative contribution to the book's identity. Much gratitude to both Milena Vassova and Conni Rosewarne for their extensive research and to Tom Howells, Phoebe Adler and Paddy Fisher for all of their writing, copy-editing and inquiry.

Thanks go to all the companies, makers and craftspeople that are featured in this book, and to all the photographers who have contributed their beautiful imagery. Without these people, this book would both not have been possible. Special thanks go to Alexander Reed, Alec Farmer, Nic Webb, Tim Chilcott, Morten Kristensen and Tom Donhou whose enthusiasm for the project and open approach to collaboration has been a driving force.

IMAGE CREDITS

cover photograph by Nick Warner

pp. 10–11, 14, 12–13, 180, photography by Jack Taylor Gotch

pp. 16–21, photography by Theres Nilsson

pp. 22–23, photography by Melissa Deerson

pp. 24–29, 60–67, 106–109, 100–101, photography by Nick Warner

p. 30, photography by Alex de Kraker

pp. 31, 32–33, photography by Niels van Loon

p. 40, photography © Jennifer Galatioto/ Greenpointers.com

pp. 6, 42–47, photography by Niall Walker

pp. 48–51, courtesy John Cho Moore

pp. 54–57, courtesy Dashing Tweeds

p. 59 left, photography by Camilla Greenwell Photography

pp. 58, 59 right, 52–53, photography by Irem Arig

p. 68, photography by Virginie Pargny

p. 69, photography by Michael Rucci

pp. 70–71, photography by Joe Rucci

pp. 78, 72–73, photography by Simon Camper

pp. 74–77, courtesy Brooklyn Glass

pp. 79, 80–81, photography by Andrew Pheby

pp. 82–85, photography by Kim Williams

pp. 86–87, 94–95, courtesy Serrote

pp. 88–93, courtesy of Awagami Factory

p. 96, courtesy Michael O'Brien

pp. 97–99, courtesy Bomo Art

pp. 2–3, 120–123, photography by Bette Walker

pp. 110–111, 116–119, 188, photography by Martin Pedersen

pp. 124–127, photography by Carolyn Carter

pp. 130–135, photography by Ace Boothby

pp. 140–141, courtesy Svante Djärv

pp. 142–147, photography by Larry Tips

pp. 148–149, courtesy Vinylize

pp. 150–157, courtesy H Huntsman & Sons

pp. 158–161, courtesy Momotaro Jeans

pp. 176–179, photography by Teemu Rytky

Designed by Amy Cooper-Wright at Black Dog Publishing.
Edited by Leanne Hayman and Nick Warner at Black Dog Publishing.

Black Dog Publishing Limited
10a Acton Street, London, WC1X 9NG
United Kingdom

Tel: +44 (0)20 7713 5097
Fax: +44 (0)20 7713 8682
info@blackdogonline.com
www.blackdogonline.com

British Library Cataloguing-in-Publication Data.
A CIP record for this book is available from the British Library.

ISBN 978 1 908966 39 1

Black Dog Publishing Limited, London, UK, is an environmentally responsible company. *Made by Hand: Contemporary Makers, Traditional Practices* is printed on sustainably sourced paper.

art design fashion
history photography
theory and things

london uk   www.blackdogonline.com